Cycles

Judy Dater

Judy Dater "Cycles"

English Edition Copyright © 1994 by Curatorial Assistance, Inc.
113 East Union St., Pasadena, Ca. 91103-3927.
Photographs Copyright © 1992 by Judy Dater.
Introduction Copyright © 1994 by Sheryl Conkelton.
"The Artist As The Two-Million-Year-Old Woman" Copyright © 1994 by
Clarissa Pinkola Estés, Ph.D. All Rights Reserved.
Texts Copyright © 1992 by Donna Stein and Michiko Kasahara.

Photographs curated by Donna Stein.
Text edited by Carolyn Coman.
Proofed by Laure Oliver and E.M. Ginger.
"Dissonance" translated by Gavin Frew.

The typeface is Cycles designed by Sumner Stone, first used in this book.
Book design by Jack W. Stauffacher of The Greenwood Press.
Color separation, printing and binding by Toppan Printing Co., Ltd.

Front cover: 56. Child/Woman, 1991
Back cover: 150. Honeymoon, 1991

Contents

Introduction

In the early 1970s I attended a women's college. Moving from a small town, where emphasis was not placed on education (or illumination of any kind), I was confronted by a very different kind of small community when I reached the campus. Self-examination – both in terms of self-scrutiny and self-motivation – was a norm; my self-consciousness found a purpose and was gradually transformed from awkwardness into awareness. In spite of its very deliberate limitation in one aspect, this community did not censure in any way. It did allow me to locate myself in a defined place in order to gain perspective and discover direction.

In the early 1970s, Judy Dater was already photographing, and the self-scrutiny and self-motivation I was beginning to discover were apparent as strong, central themes in her work. In her early pictures there is a definite sense of the artist seeking – not like some, to discover only her own reflection, but to locate a sense of her own sufficient self. Like my small college environment, Dater's photographing within her own experience provided a platform from which to launch a series of thoughtful explorations of self, consciousness and place in the world.

The motifs in some of Dater's early images – a submerged deer, the directed male gaze, the entwined bodies of lovers – each express some aspect of her consciousness and are meant to be read as visual equivalents for transitory states of mind and emotion. In others, her own body is a symbol of female being, providing human counterpart to upright columns and uplifting branches. Sometimes she is carefully draped to hide both her identity and her sexuality and deny the desire to equate knowledge of these two aspects.

Dater also photographed other people, many of them women who looked into the camera from her own world, each portraying in her strength of character a possible role, a potential model of a way to be. In none of them do the women seem exposed or naked as people do when their clothes have been taken off. In none of them is sexuality the result of the projections of the photographer. Instead, the powerful emotions of these women are channeled in the opposite direction, from subject to photographer and thus to viewer, rather than viewer to object. Each subject is resolutely her own creation, the portrait offered to, not taken by, the camera.

Ironically, Dater's images of men made during this time are more wide-ranging in the revelation of attitude toward their subjects. While each of the women in her respective portrait is a knowable individual, this is true of only some of her photographs of men. Many of the male portraits are of photographers and other photography-world individuals Dater knew, and these images project a sense of personality very well. But in others, Dater depicts not the person but the male form, much in the way she had used her own body in earlier images, as a symbolic entity or cipher. The body – this time male – becomes the artist's muse in an elegant role reversal.

In the early 1980s Dater produced a body of work that moved away from the interior and the symbolic. Influenced by a growing awareness of the dominion of the social contract over individual effort, she produced a series of images in which she played out some of the roles proposed for women. In patently artificial and minimal settings, Dater donned absurd costumes and handled what were in actuality everyday objects but became, in her combinations, outlandish props. Each character promoted some role to the exclusion of others; in different images Dater reduced herself to whore or housekeeper, witch, superwoman, or caged bird. In rude and garish colors she disguised herself and her interiority by portraying herself as a series of social constructions: flat and without depth or alternative. In this attempt to deal straightforwardly with identity dictated from without, Dater created deeply ironic pictures and made perhaps the strongest and most direct statement of her resistance to such ideas.

Aside from this particular investigation Dater

remained emphatically grounded in her exploration of self-realized identity. She continued to work obsessively with the nude self-portrait, depicting her figure in badlands, in grasslands, in flat lands, in salt flats. Often reclining but just as often upright and active, she shows herself with nature's equivalents: earth, vegetation, a stone, a rock. Often faceless and deliberately without a sense of scale or exact location she is depicted in this series more as a natural element than as the individual Judy Dater.

In her photographs from the late 1980s, Dater created portraits of people no longer still but moving, evaporating into blurs of light. She constructed complex pieces for her series *Memories* in which the emotions of others shift and flicker across multiple images. Actions are turned into choreographed movements, and objects, such as teacups and lawn sprinklers, ever so slightly set askew, are transformed into mythical vessels and water carriers. Motion altered the sense of icon found in her earlier work; timelessness and symbolic stillness gave way to immediacy and flux. There is a sense, too, of meaning becoming more layered, more individual and idiosyncratic, and less the easily understood language of Western symbols. Even though Dater employed the often-used strategy of multiple parts, the meaning of these works remain fluid and unspecified: these works do not resolve easily. They are, instead, meant to remain open, to resonate with possibilities beyond specific notions.

Fragments take on a coherence as parts of a whole. The large patterns are revealed, the cycles become apparent, the meaningful obsessions are sorted out from the merely self-indulgent, and coincidences and parallels can be seen as significant. In retrospect, Dater's oeuvre parallels the particular development of photography in this country during a specific generation as much as it can be assigned a place within the unfolding of American feminism. Whether it is described in these terms or called these names does not alter its tenets or its evolution. Dater's work shares the power of female perspectives, such as the compelling immediacy of Diane Arbus' portraits and the uninhibited use of the female body in Carolee Schneemann's performances as surely as her shift from straightforward depiction of photographic narration reflects the changing temper of photographic representation.

Like Arbus and Schneemann and many others, Dater creates images to explore her own potential, discover her own possibilities. Her art is a representation of her own history, based on actual events, gleaned from people she knows, expressed in a pictorial language that is grounded in sensate experience. It offers some alternative to the authoritarian and too-distanced historical view. It shows Dater to be, paradoxically, both singularly brave and emblematic of a generation.

Sheryl Conkelton
New York

The Artist As
The Two-Million-Year-Old Woman

*Within every woman there is a wild and natural crea-
ture, a powerful force filled with good instincts, passion-
ate creativity and ageless knowing.* * This is an apt
definition of a gifted woman, and Judy Dater fits the
description very well. And further, by way of her cho-
sen creative form – photography – she resonates to
the two-million-year-old woman found in fairy tales.
Like the Baba Yaga, the old Nature Mother who lives
at the center of the forest stirring her pots of bones
and flesh – not consuming but creating the bodies
anew – Dater stirs and renews images that are old
beyond time.

Dater does not shy away from the artist's most
difficult work. The artist's greatest challenge is not
just to record images, but far more: to redeem the
forgotten parts of life itself, to revive the moments
and gestures of humanity that carry passion and
vitality. This is what separates the artist from the pre-
tender. The artist hauls, pulls, dives and strives to
bring back from the brink, or from the abyss, whatever humans have lost and forgotten, whatever has
been misused, trivialized unjustly or demeaned,
whatever remains endangered.

Like the daughter of Bilam Chilam, the great jaguar
priest of the Mayan race who saved the world by
inhaling all the people and things in it, an artist like
Dater *lives the images,* is clearly filled with both the
lavish and lean shapes, and all the sizes of the land,
the animal world and all the people in their primal
and properly startling sentience.

What do we really mean when we say a person car-
ries artistic vision? That she is filled with millions of
hands and legs and elbows, hillocks, chasms and
deserts, horses, lakes and flying things. That she is in
love with all shapes and forms, all light and shadow,
all corners, all interstices, all open mesas. That the
curve of the arch of a foot can tear a cry out of her

*Clarissa Pinkola Estés, Ph.D. *Women Who Run With the Wolves.*
New York: Ballantine Books, 1992.

6

chest. That the violet haze just now hovering over a pond can make her insane with the need to show it to someone, to feast on it with another soul.

The artist knows in her bones that the images she brings forth are not solely for her pleasure; that they need be born because they carry some remedy, some beauty, some mending, some shaking, creating or vitality into a world that is often too busy dying to notice its spent condition or its spiritual needs. In the old healing folklore of my family, there is a belief that images and ideas are living beings with minds and intentions of their own; that these seek entry into the world in order to enliven, repair, inspire, make possible an integration of dark and light, and to advance the destiny of humans.

The overall name for the force behind this phenomenon of image-and-idea-making is called *El duende*: the unseen force behind creative action. In this tradition, the person who can translate between the inner and outer worlds, who is bilingual in the languages of images and of art, that one is called *La Maestra.* She, like Dater, is the one who has mastered and bridged the span between the mythic and mundane worlds, forsaking neither, not exalting one over the other, but fully empowered in each.

This is why artists can never submit their visions to society's sanction; either its approval or its disapproval. The intense human need to preserve a deep symbolic life through the making of and the experiencing of images and ideas is an incontestable psychological fact. Yet we live in a culture that often attempts to undermine that necessity in ever so many ways. In our time, an artist like Dater does double duty. The artist must not only occupy the place in the psyche, the headwaters of the pysche so to speak, where the inner and outer worlds, night and day dreams merge, where spirit and body are undivided, but she also *must* express whatever images step onto her psychic stage. Whether she understands them, fears them, is stunned by them, regardless, she must assume they all carry worthy meaning.

Acts of vibrant art are very dangerous works indeed. The artist must be of stalwart faith, and must possess, even if outside of complete consciousness, a sense of Selfhood that is unassailable, as well as a good set of either *ovarios* or *cojones*. An artist may be able to produce the images, but may not be able to explain them or even comprehend them until long, long after. We may have to only feel them, be stirred by them, ask questions of ourselves and of them. We may have to practice listening for answers. If over many meetings with the images, an individual is able to begin shedding the light of consciousness on them, so be it. But, more often than not, most of the images brought forth will never be completely analyzable. Therefore, and blessedly, they will continue to carry an immense numinosity, that is, the ability to stir us deeply and forever.

That is the essence of the artist's work, the intense kind of work that Dater does not shrink from. One might argue that it is one of society's functions to desacralize everything it touches. All the more reason for artists to insist on taking every opportunity to muster up every and any image that comes to them. An artist knows that the society of spirits, daimons, boogeys and saints in the collective unconscious are the *only* mediators of art that have any sense whatsoever, the only ones who can be relied upon for any kind of guidance at all. Though we may wrestle with the inner figures, and they or we may attempt to subdue one another, or burst each other apart to find out the actual attributes at the core of the idea, the images that arise beyond the ego are completely honest. They have no false propriety, no adherence to prevailing custom, no labels. Only meaning: intense, vast and undiluted. Delivered right into our gullets, laps, hearts or minds for us to comprehend, admit, balance.

In Dater's work are images that may provoke many feelings. Some of her images may feed, shock, awaken, strengthen, cause us to rise up or to swoon, re-create memory, or arouse. From the practice of *curanderisma,* the old healing arts in my family, there is a saying, "If something is astonishing, look closer, there is more soul to it than one thinks." In analytical psychology, there is a similar theory – if something – an image, an event, a person – is arresting, it is also numinous, that is, in some way it contains a strong spiritual component. Dater's images carry all of these. The wild and natural image of a light shining between a woman's legs as she stands on an aureole of earth; the woman nude in all her variant skin: rough, smooth, striated, veined, dimpled, bony, mounded, yielding; the woman who has become part of an ancient pictograph, part three-dimensional, part bas relief, both rising and sinking into the stone; the double set of eyes in the belly of the naked black man; and the blackest black man seated next to the whitest white teacup in the world. They are in their own ways, and depending on the viewer, shocking, arresting, startling. And all to the good.

Women have been shocking for centuries. How? Just by being their usual creative selves. There is a force at the center of the feminine nature that is so massively spiritual, so powerfully moving, so hair-raising, so eternal and ecstatic, so life-giving, so inspiring – that humans from Dante to Goethe, from Poe to Jung, imagined the feminine nature as the end all and be all, the central soul figure of all men, the soul of the world itself, the Sofia, the Tara, the Sita, the Shekinah, the Omnapiscus. To harness this as Dater has, to envision life through the numinous feminine nature, to actualize it in everyday life through images like hers, has a disassembling and revisioning effect on ideas that adhere to a tired or unexamined status quo.

In this way, the artist's images have the ability to break up stony, unplantable ground in the collective psyche, while creating new soft ground for the planting of new ideas. In this way, the cycle of life and death and rebirth that is central to the feminine nature is the great heart of all image-making. The wild, untamed, instinctive knowing, passion and creativity in Dater's photographs are not only images, they are evidence; evidence of her deep diving into the unconscious, the place where only the very brave can go, and return. That place that has no words like "success," that place that does not care for a biography nor for what dates the artist married or went here or there, but only that one night she set out alone into the desert, deeper and deeper she walked, and then sat on the sand under the billion stars, waiting and wanting, until suddenly from out of her heart or her mouth, or perhaps from the palm of her hand, burst a blood-red blossom, opening for an instant in the night, offering only a moment to register its image before it folded into itself and was gone. That an artist does this, that she *can* do this, that she can stand it, bear it, that she can bring back to the mundane world what she once saw fleetingly in another world, *that* is the artist's great gift. That is Judy Dater's great gift, and irrevocably so.

Clarissa Pinkola Estés, Ph.D.
Cheyenne, Wyoming

Portfolio of Photographs

1. My hands, Death Valley, 1980

2. Self-portrait,1965

13

3. Self-portrait in rain,1982

4. Self-portrait, Patmos,1991

5. Self-portrait with parents,1981

6. Self-portrait, Craters of the Moon, 1981

7. Self-portrait with mist, 1980

8. Self-portrait in grasslands,1981

9. Self-portrait, Badlands,1981

10. Self-portrait at Salt Flats,1981

11. Self-portrait with stone,1981

12. Self-portrait with white rock, 1983

13. Self-portrait holding up rock,1983

35

14. Self-portrait with sparkler, 1980

15. Self-portrait with petroglyph,1981

39

16. Self-portrait, Arles, France,1973

17. Self-portrait with mask, 1981

18. Self-portrait on deserted road,1982

19. Cat woman,1982

20. Twinka Thiebaud, actress, model,1970

21. Nehemiah,1975

22. Marianne with mask,1972

23. Belle de Jour, 1986

24. Aarmour Starr,1972

25. Libby,1971

26. Untitled (Alabaster statue),1964

27. Kathleen and China,1972

28. Maggie in church,1986

29. Stephania,1988

30. Japanese bath,1991

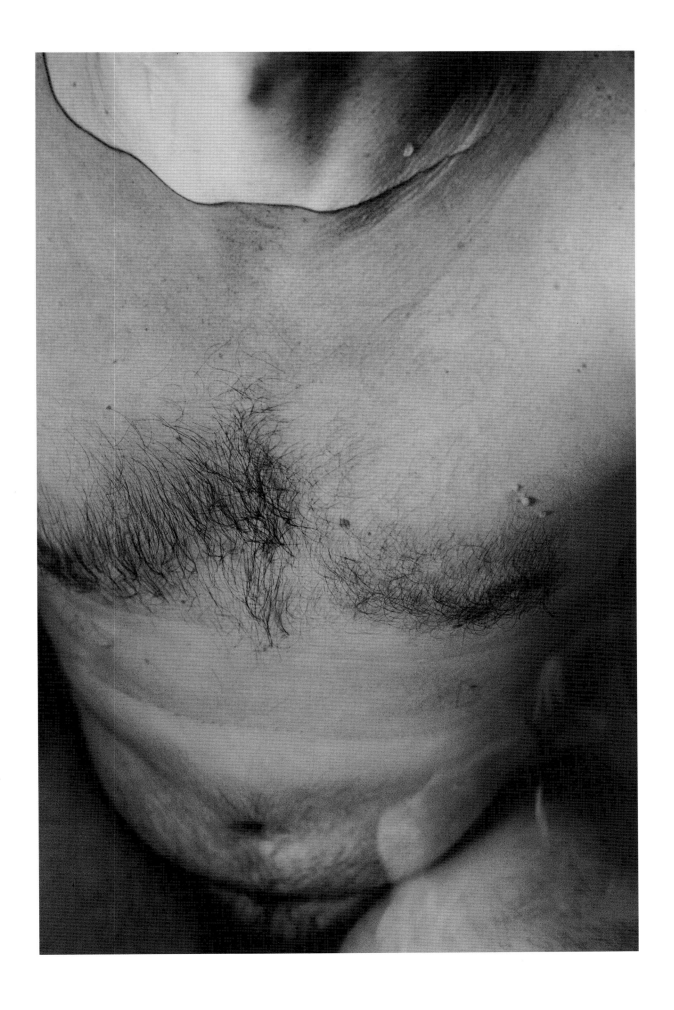

31. Dead deer in pond, 1966

32. Summer bath, 1975

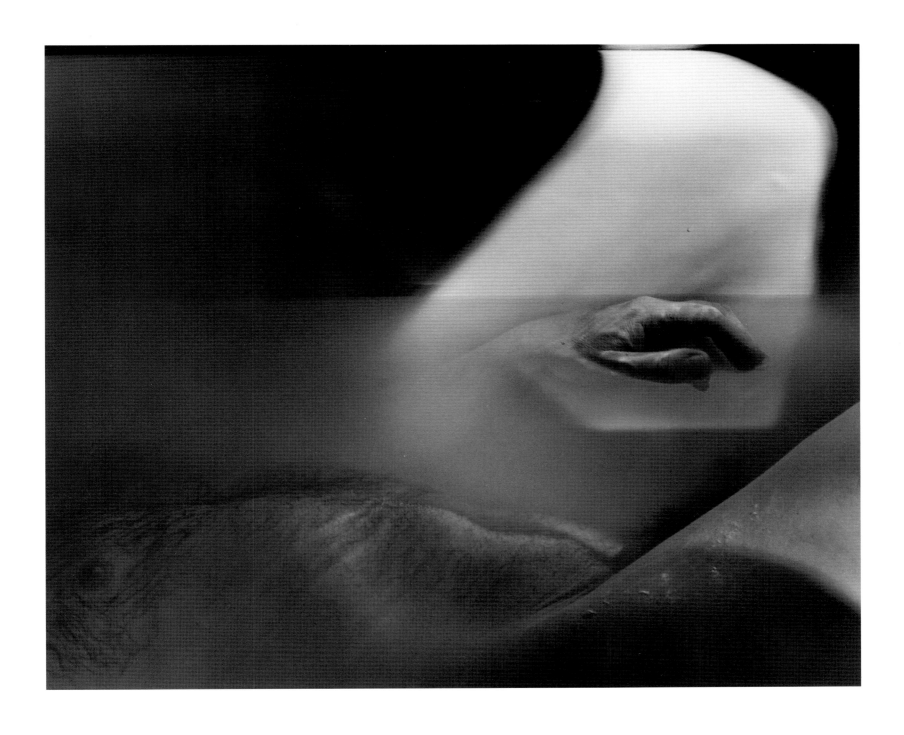

33. Male nude in mirror with hat, 1991

34. Double trouble, Paris,1991

35. Offering #1, 1988

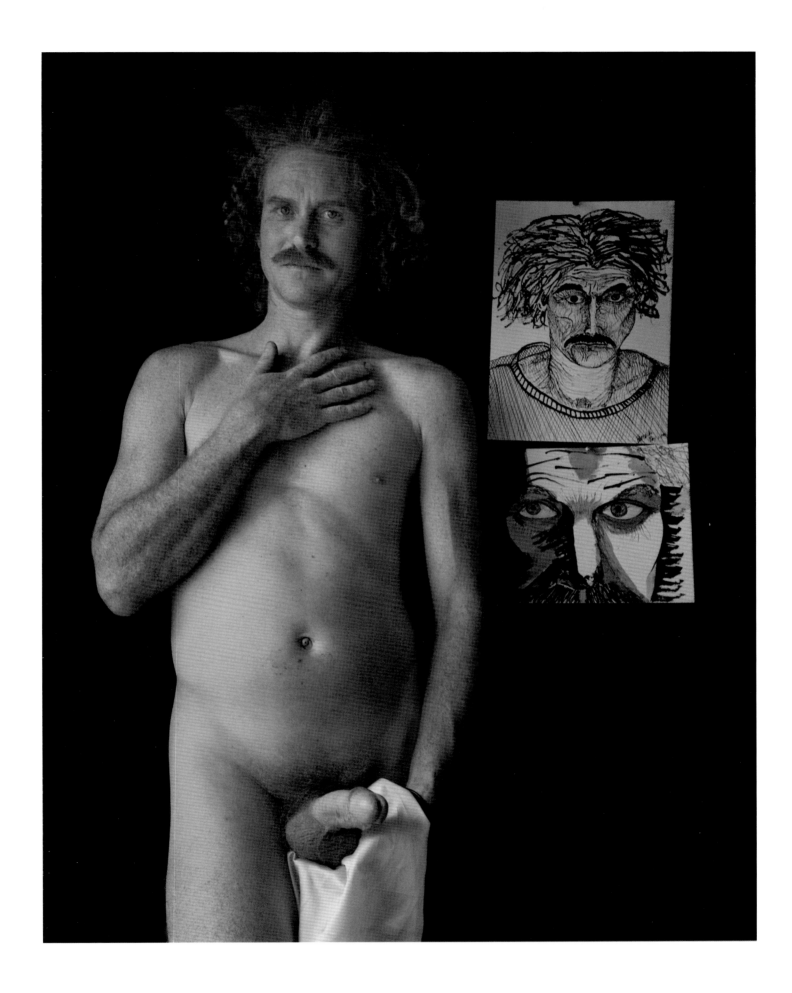

36. Gwen (torso),1972

37. Walter Chappell,1977

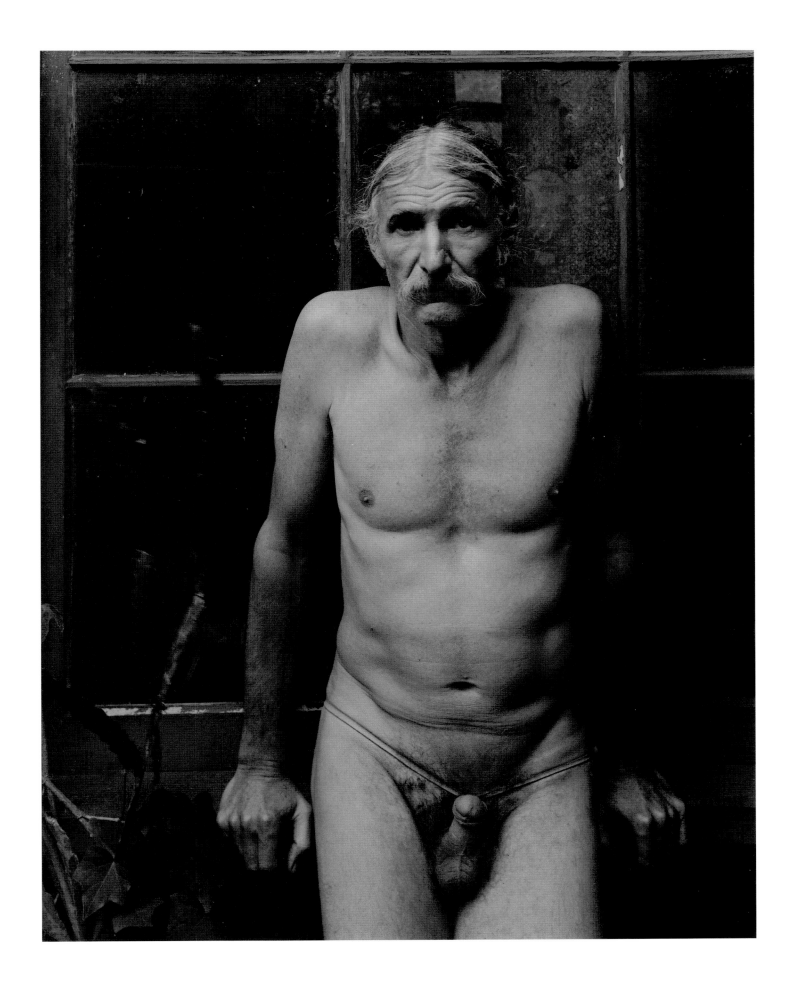

38. Chris,1975

39. Prayer, 1971

40. Jack with monkey,1973

41. Edmund Teske,1978

42. Maureen with fan, 1972

43. Memory #1,1987

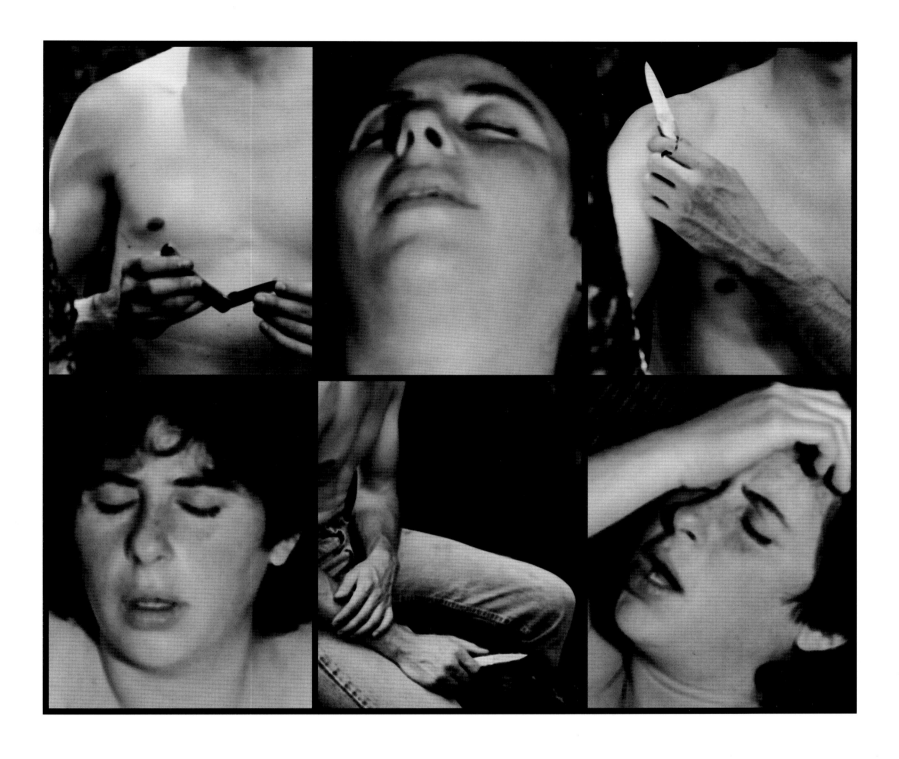

44. Memory #2,1988

45. Memory #4, 1988

46. The city,1989

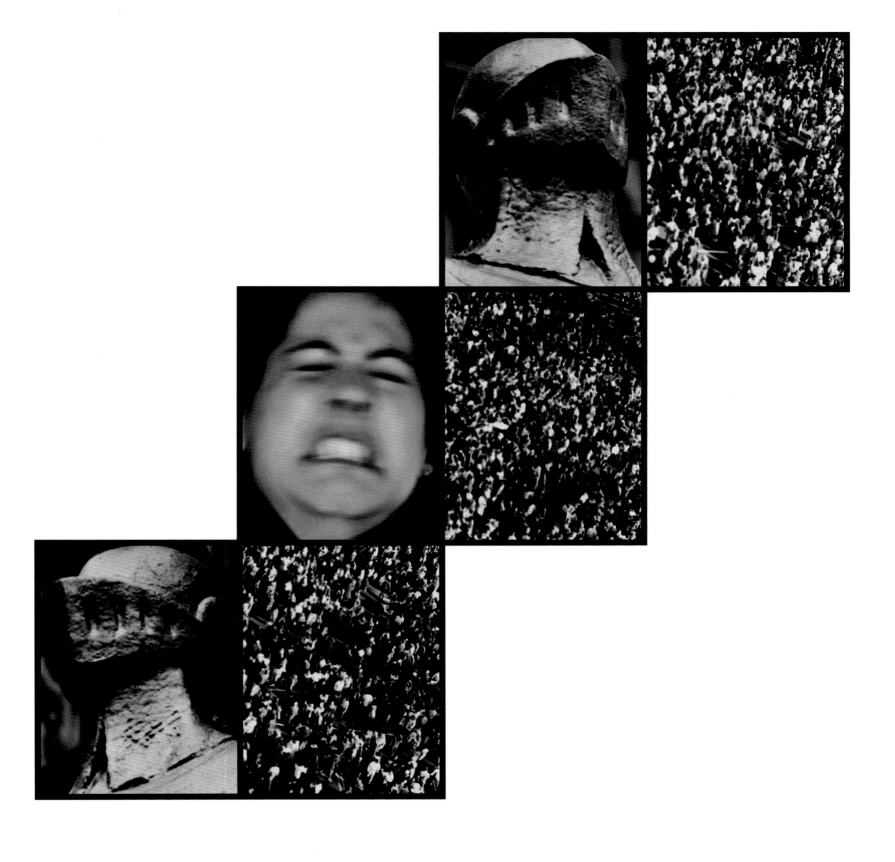

47. The meaning of life,1989

48. Playing with fire,1989

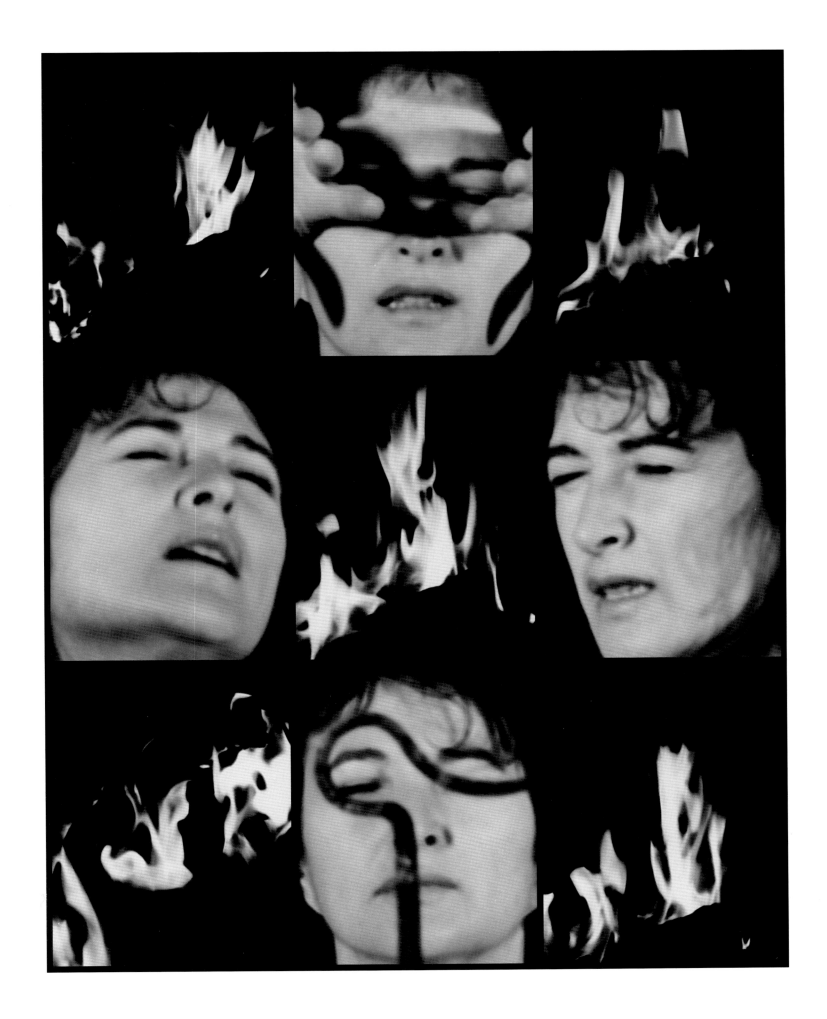

49. End of innocence,1989

50. Cycles, 1989

51. Cycles (detail),1989

52. Cycles (detail),1989

53a.

53b.

54. The pond,1990

53c.

53a, 53b, 53c. Blue angel,1990

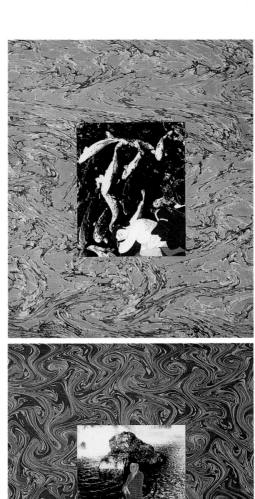

55. The pond (detail),1990

56. Child/Woman,1991

57. Self-portrait with party dress,1982

58. Pregnant dream,1968-69

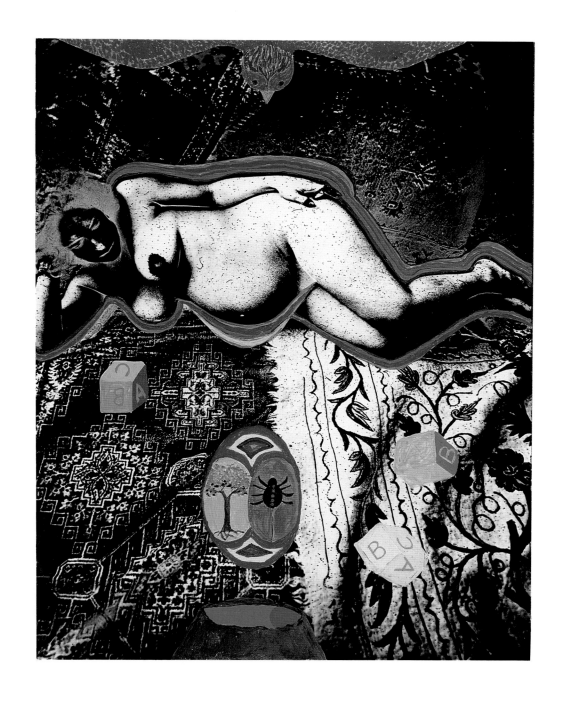

59a.

59b.

60. Queen of the night,1982

59c.

59a, 59b, 59c. Oracle, 1984

61. Elephant woman steps out, 1982

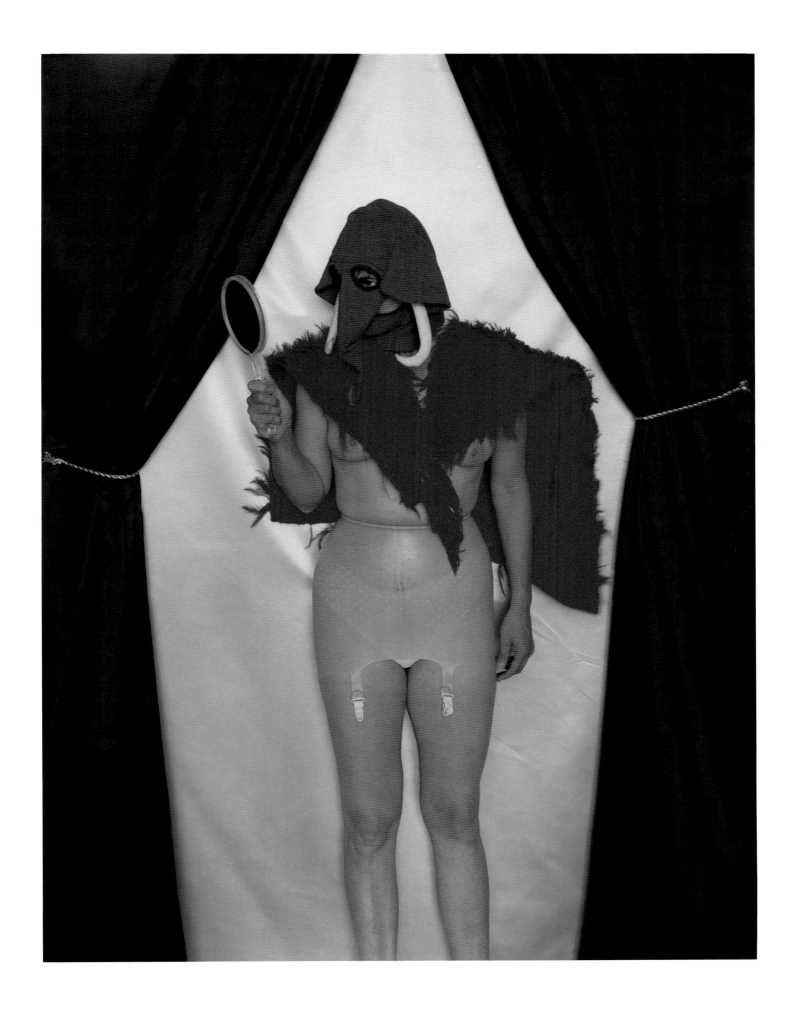

62. Spider woman, 1982

63. Scream,1982

64. Death by ironing,1982

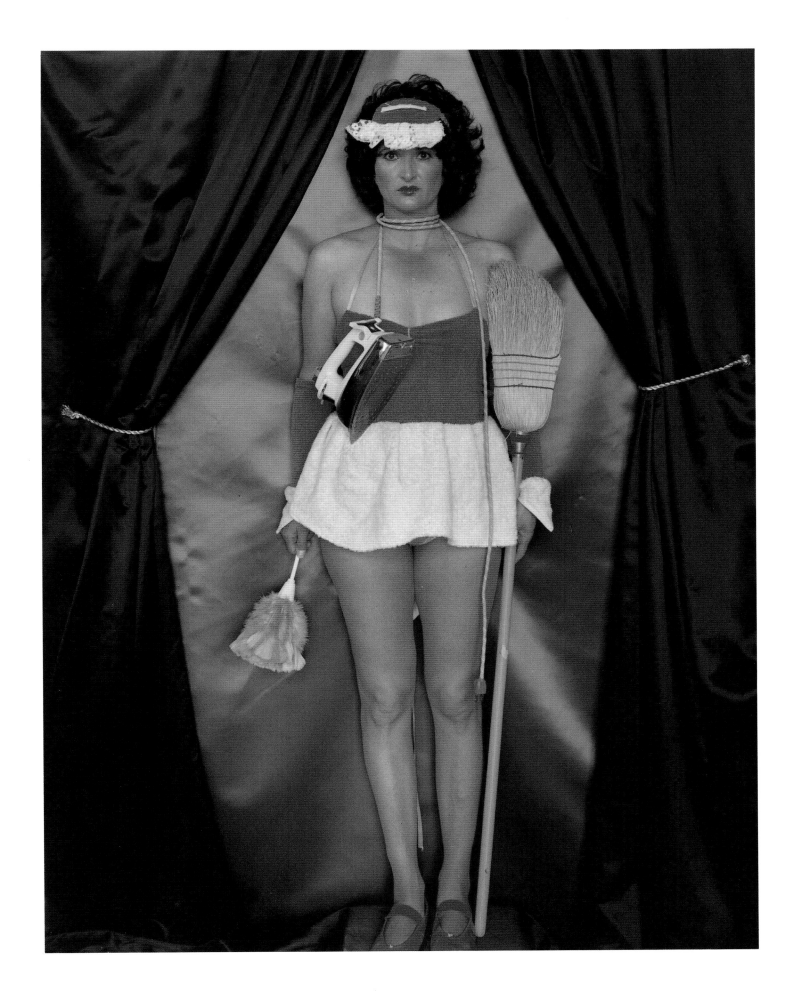

65. Eating,1982

66. The magician,1982

67. All-American nude,1982

68. Self-portrait with Bugs Bunny,1982

69. Fourth of July, State #4, 1984

70. New York window, 1991

In the summertime there was an old woman who always seemed to be at her window in her underwear. She was usually absentmindedly toying with her blinds and gazing at the street. I would sit and sip my capuccino and watch her and wonder what she did all day and what she had done for her life, and how long she had been living in that apartment. It seemed very lonely and very boring and very scary. It made me wonder how different my life was from hers. Would I end up an old woman gazing out the window for the end of my life? After watching her for a month or two I bought some lace curtains so that I could look out but no one could look in at me. I painted the windows a beautiful turquoise blue. The windows are arched at the top and have alot of character to them. They are old fashioned and somehow european. The turquoise color makes me think of New Mexico. When I look at them I sometimes forget that I am in New York.

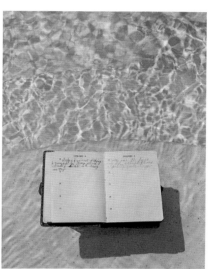

154

71. Teenage diary,1982

72. Teenage diary (detail),1982

155

73. Love letters #3,1984

74. Love letters #3 (detail),1984

75. Love letters #3 (detail),1984

76. I didn't want to but I did,1991

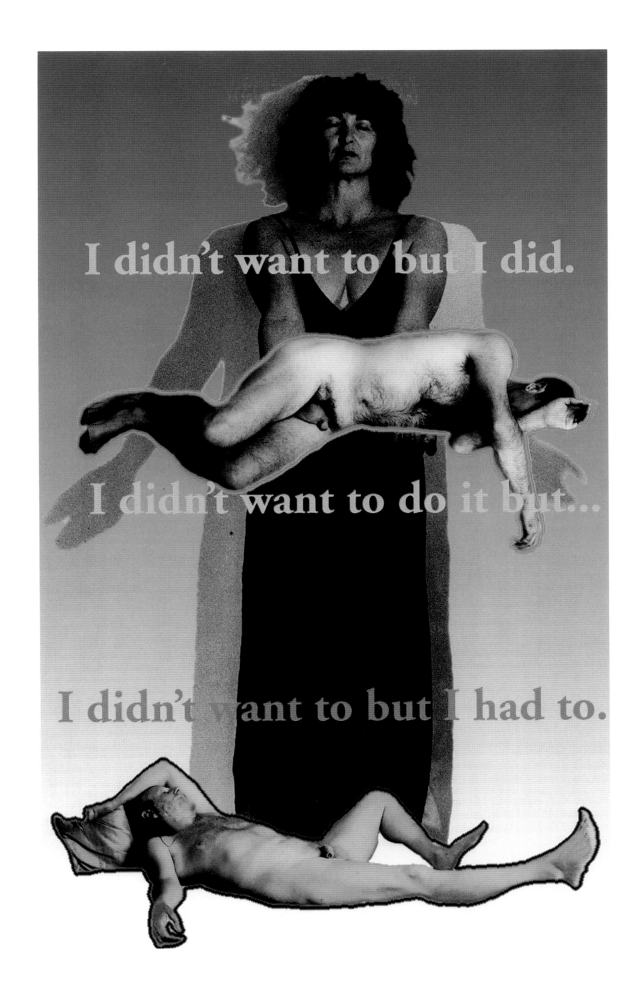

77. Viewing Mt. Rushmore,1982

78. Man with horse's skull, 1979

79. Man at pond, Tuscarora, Nevada,1979

173

80. Nude at Ship Rock, 1979

81.Chris with tea cup,1978

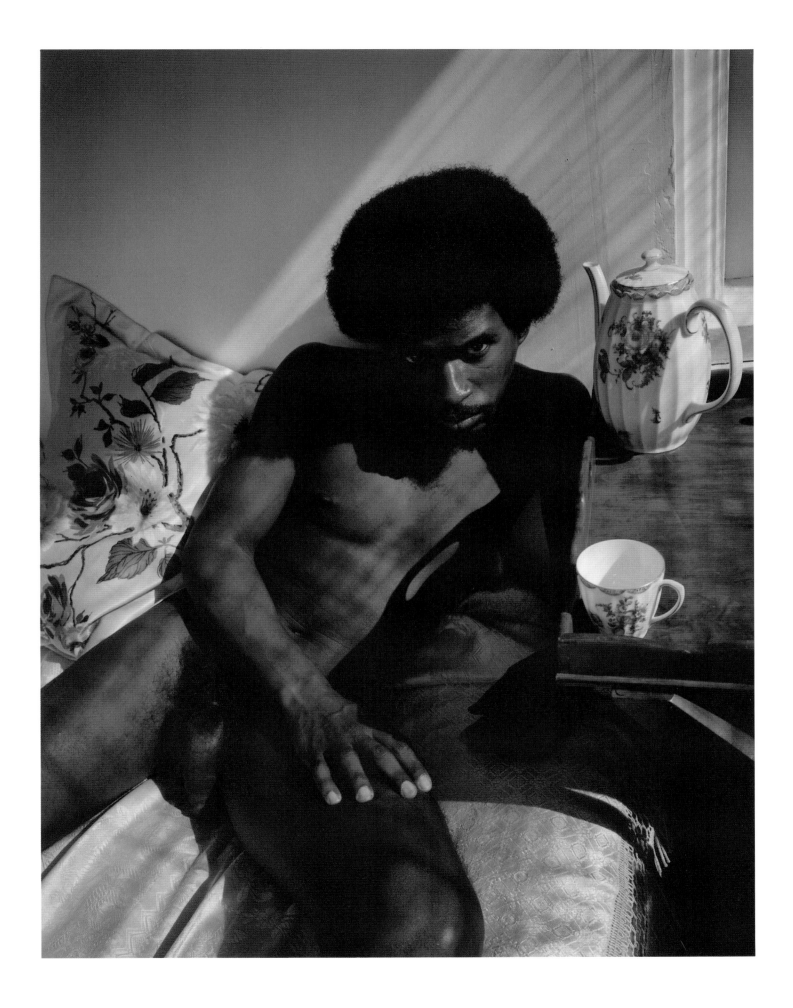

177

82. Mark Johnstone,1983

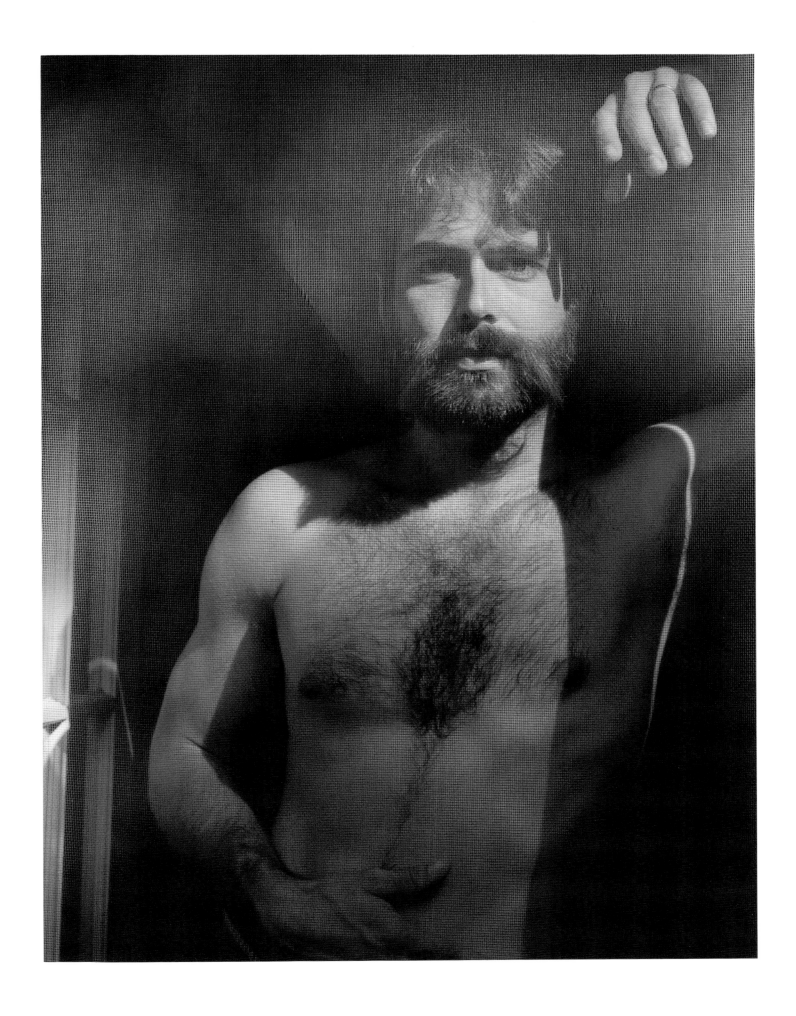

83. Bill Justima,1980

84. Ralph with radish, 1979

85. Kamal El Mallakh,1980

86. Vickie Singer, 1986

87. Man with bulldogs, New York,1976

189

88. Solo, Hawaii, 1978

89. Postmen, Arles,1976

90. Peter Bunnell, 1977

91. Minor White,1975

92. Lucia,1972

93. Linda with blackbird,1975

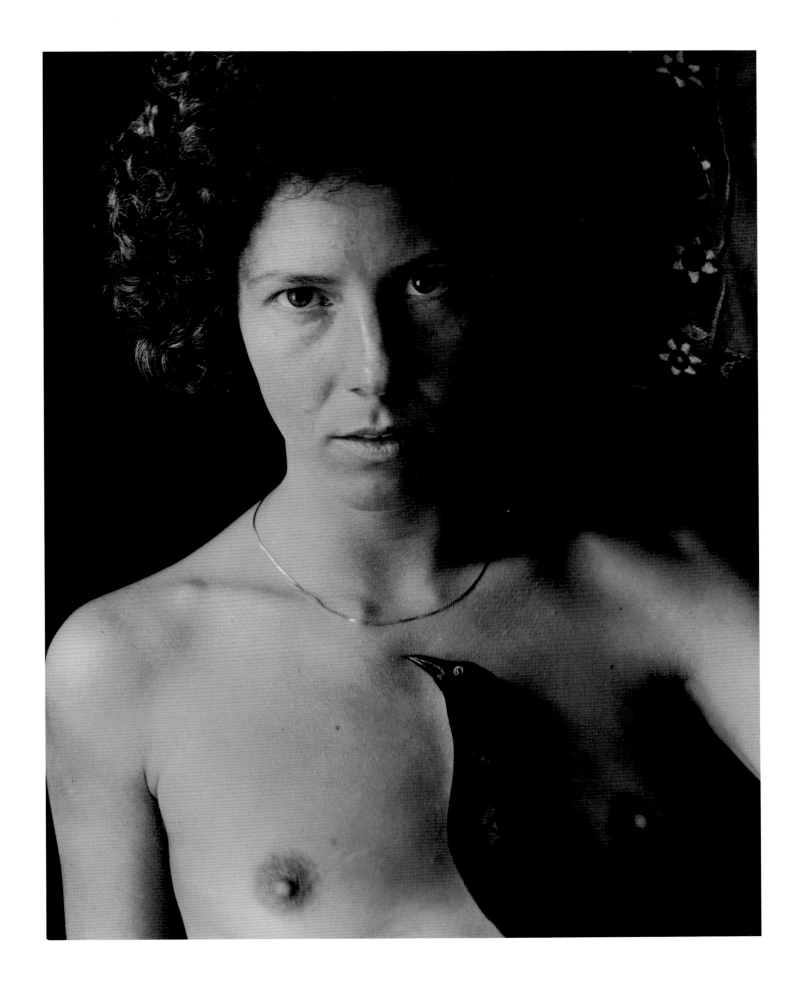

94. Linda's dream, 1975

203

95. Double heart tree, 1975

96. Consuelo Cloos, 1980

97. John Gutmann, 1975

98. Priest, Tomales, California, 1966

99. The voyeur, 1968

100. Imogen and Twinka at Yosemite,1974

Between Light and Dark
An Interview with Judy Dater

Donna Stein

DS   Do you consider yourself a photographer?

JD   Like all art photographers, I prefer to think of myself as an artist. I have worked with painting, collage, multiples, and the computer. Occasionally, I still enjoy straight photography.

DS   Is there a continuous thread linking your earliest images to your contemporary expressions?

JD   I am interested in human beings and human nature, theater and role playing, costume and disguise, humor, psychology, sexuality, romance and stories, the dark side of things, the cosmic. I want to explore the subterranean, hidden side of myself. I am intrigued by the transformative quality of light. I am also interested in realism, the idea that sometimes truth is stranger than fiction. I want to know the nature of things. I believe everything I've mentioned weaves in and out of my work.

DS   Do you begin with a concept or an image?

JD   My creative process is a composite event and encompasses whatever is going on – dreams, revelations, psychiatry, talk, something I saw in a movie, a passage from a book. It rarely involves one specific experience, but comes from a combination of sources. I most often start with an image. Ideas are present, but in a latent form, imbedded in my subconscious. The images function like keys, unlocking hidden thoughts. Perhaps on some subliminal level, I know more about what I'm trying to say than I care to verbalize or even admit. I make visual selections, which help me get at these dormant ideas. Because my subconscious is always altering its focus, the visual keys keep changing.

DS   Is content more important in your work than visual elements such as light, space, and graphic design?

JD   Content would probably be at the top of my list, though subject matter is worthless unless all the other visual elements hang together.

DS   What role does free association play in your conceptualization process?

JD   It has a very big role. Free association is related to intuition and I have an innate sense about things. These feelings and ideas occur spontaneously, usually when I'm actually photographing. I see something out of the corner of my eye or a subject will say a word that triggers a long stream of thoughts about what I want to do. I try to maintain this heightened sense of awareness while working, because it allows me to act on the smallest detail.

DS   Are you aware of your motivation and interpretation of images while you're photographing or is it only later that you realize what you have done?

JD   Probably a bit of both. I'm not a hundred percent cognizant of what I'm doing. It's like dreaming – you sense meaning – but when you recount your dream the next day you piece together symbols in an effort to analyze its meaning. After I've gained some distance from the work it's easier to identify what's truly contained in a given picture.

DS   How specific do you want your images to be in relation to your personal history?

JD   I want the photographs to evoke my feelings about personal history, but I don't want them to be specific or journalistic. I have tried to face myself as honestly as possible and I hope that inspires my viewers to do the same. I realize confrontation may not be a pleasant experience and may cause people to back off. That's why I try to seduce viewers, coax them into wanting to look, and hopefully they discover something unexpected or useful. I also want to entertain and amaze.

DS   Do you also want to shock?

JD   Absolutely. I've always wanted to shock people with my work. I've consciously tried to be provocative and disturbing, to wake people up. I don't try to offend, but some viewers misunderstand.

DS   Do you consider yourself a witness or a participant?

JD   I think I'm a participant first, and then a witness. The work comes from my own experience and reflects what's going on in my life at the moment. To create art, I must detach myself from the personal and become a witness of my own experiences.

DS   Do you consider your portraits psychological and therefore interpretive revelations of character?

JD   Yes. I think they are very psychological, because I'm trying to capture a complex spectrum of emotions. What a model projects psychologically is more important than whether I achieve a good likeness. I like visually flamboyant people who communicate strong, universal emotions. Some people naturally convey their interior life better than others.

DS   Can you generalize about the typical qualities you look for in a model?

JD   I've never been particularly interested in beauty in the classic sense. It doesn't have anything to do with whether a model is physically attractive or not. Of course, some of the people I photograph like *Nehemiah* (#21), are beautiful, but in general, I'm interested in people with style and energy. I don't know if people have different kinds and colors of auras or even if I believe in them, but that's a good way to describe what I sense. I try to capture these transcendent qualities in photographs so other people can see them too.

DS   Do you consciously manipulate people in front of the camera?

JD   I consciously try to seize an unusual feature that exemplifies the subterranean qualities I want to probe. The face is more than a map, it's a person's soul.

DS   Is the photographic portrait a record of the sitter's personality or a projection of a photographer's fantasy?

JD   If ten photographers used the same model, each photographer would react to distinctive aspects of personality and setting and would certainly reveal another side of the individual. I'm more interested in my personal fantasy about a model than in making a record of who she or he is, because often we've barely met and there's no chance for me to experience who they are. All I know is what I see so I follow my instincts.

DS   How have changes in equipment affected your interpretation of subjects?

JD   I dabbled around with the 35 mm and 2¼ for the first year or two. Then I started using a Deardorff 4 x 5 camera, which had a significant impact on my portraits. In this day and age, a large format view camera is a novelty. It's an impressive object, which I definitely use as a dramatic prop. Models respond differently to it than they do to a smaller camera. It's time consuming squaring up the composition in the back of the camera, standing under a big black cloth, making all the settings on the lens, and putting in the film holder. The upside-down image reflected on the ground glass helps me abstract what I am photographing. Because I can't work quickly, I spend a lot of time with the subjects and can draw things out of them. The negative the 4 x 5 produces is bigger, resulting in more beautiful prints with finer tones and less grain. I try to capitalize on these sensual surfaces.

DS   Are your concerns more feminine than masculine?

JD   I think my concerns are extremely personal. I pay careful attention to the way people act around me, both male and female. Being a woman has influenced the way I think and feel. Nevertheless, I have a very strong masculine side. I'm very independent.

DS   Do your portraits use costume to suggest personality?

JD   Whatever a person happens to have on at the moment is a costume. The same person could dress in ten outfits and each one would present another side of her personality. I automatically gravitate toward mythic representations. That's why it's not essential I capture the individual. It's also why I don't like to photograph famous people, like John Wayne or Albert Einstein, because their celebrity and eminence get in the way. When I photograph unknown people they can represent concepts larger than themselves.

DS   How do the psychologically challenging portrayals in your photographs differ from earlier photographers?

JD   Early photographers like Julia Margaret Cameron, Nadar or Carjat made intense, riveting, and penetrating portraits. I appreciate the solidity and solemnity they attained in their portraiture as well as the graphic structure of their compositions. I wanted to achieve a similar effect. Yet, most other nineteenth-century photographers depicted people looking off into the distance, not at the camera, because photographers thought looking straight at the camera was less flattering and looking into the distance more romantic. From the beginning, I made a conscious decision to have my models stare into the camera. I want the viewer to confront the model face to face. This is especially true with the nudes, even though there are a few examples where a nude is faceless like *Gwen (Torso)* (#36) or *Nehemiah's Back*. I don't want the audience only to be a voyeur; they must interact with the image and put themselves in the place of the unclothed person – because when you're nude, you're more vulnerable. That attitude was never an agenda of the nineteenth-century photographer, but it has always been mine.

DS   When did your interest in voyeurism begin?

JD   When I was very young, I came across a reproduction of Thomas Hart Benton's painting, "Persephone," in a book my parents owned called *Great American Paintings* . It showed an old farmer peeking around a tree at a voluptuous nude who was oblivious to the leering old man. I spent many hours staring at that painting. It seemed so erotic and forbidding. At the age of five I'm sure I didn't have a clue what was so compelling, but my innocent young heart responded. Years later, one of my first realizations as a photographer was that taking pictures seemed synonymous with photographing the nude.

I did many nude self-portraits right from the start. Sometimes my friends would pose for me in the nude. As a college art student I took numerous classes in life drawing, which I loved, and art history. My art history classes taught me the nude was always a legitimate subject. It made sense to transfer that knowledge to photography. The camera, of course, is the perfect voyeuristic tool. It allowed me to do things I could never achieve with other media. When searching for ways I could pose and photograph the nude, I recalled Benton's "Persephone." It seemed much more interesting to place the nude in an erotic drama rather than pose him or her as a pear or landscape. Persephone, a classical theme, seemed perfect. As early as 1966 with *Legion of Honor* (#104) I started experimenting with the composition. Then in 1968, I made *The Voyeur* (#99) in which an older, dressed man is peering into a bedroom, where a nude pregnant woman is sitting in an armchair, totally unaware of the intruder. In both cases there is an older, clothed person, either male or female, looking at an unclothed young female. In *Aspen* (#106) 1969, I used a dog looking in a screen door at an unaware nude female. I had always thought the dog in that picture represented "man," but perhaps it is also me, searching for who and what I am as a woman. I've used dogs in my pictures on a few occasions and I often dream about them. A psychiatrist once told me when I dream of dogs they're subconsciously serving as my alter ego. This theme culminated with *Imogen and Twinka at Yosemite* (#100) in 1974. By then, my consciousness about the symbolic meaning of the subject matter had evolved and I made what I thought was an interesting twist to the scenario. The characters were both women, youth and old age, confronting and startled by each other. Much of the erotic charge of "Persephone" is gone, but my picture is humorous. The latest version is *Looking and Seeing*, where I am nude photographing a nude man. As reflected in a mirror, I'm looking at him through the lens and he returns the gaze to me and the viewer.

DS   Did you ever try and repeat an earlier photographer's compositions?

JD   Imogen Cunningham and Edward Weston's portraits have always been important to me. I tried to make a few photographs in the manner of Edward Weston, particularly the close-up headshots of people in Mexico. I can't think of an image that comes directly from Imogen, but ideas in her work influenced me. I always admired the way she used props – funny, mysterious objects would appear in her photographs that had a life of their own.

DS   Was *Linda's Dream* (#94) inspired by Cunningham's arranged still lifes like *The Unmade Bed*?

JD   I've owned that photograph since the early 1970s and looked at it often. I'm sure it had some effect.

DS   Did you discuss ideas about composition, attitude toward other artists, lifestyle with Imogen Cunningham?

JD   Imogen was an important role model. She photographed people whereas most of the other West Coast photographers concentrated on landscape. Imogen did a variety of subjects, which I really enjoyed. We never talked about composition. I showed her my work occasionally and she would make cryptic remarks. She never had much to say about my work, although I sensed she respected and admired me. She never praised easily. The only two people I remember her saying a good word about were Paul Strand and Edward Curtis. She worked as an assistant to Curtis very early in her career. She didn't like to talk about the f.64 or dwell on the past. She was always making sarcastic remarks and poking fun at Alfred Steiglitz, Edward Weston, and Ansel Adams. She was shocked and horrified by Diane Arbus' images. Imogen was interested in what she was doing at the moment and what she was going to do in the future, which I found inspiring. It was startling to realize a person of her age and accomplishments wasn't really interested in the past.

DS   Who else was important to you?

JD   I really admire the straightforwardness of August Sander's photographs. His portraits were simple and expressive. His character types reveal themselves through their body posture, the expression on their faces, and their clothing. *Man with Bulldogs* (#87), taken in New York, is as close as anything I've done to an August Sander because it personifies a typical man on the street. I like Man Ray's photographs a lot. Although not many of my pictures reflect his influence, I did several solarizations after looking at his work. Wynn Bullock is another photographer I really admire, especially the way he incorporates sexual tension into his compositions with nudes. The first photograph I collected was by Bullock. I always admired the strange mystical light Minor White captured. Movies have always been a big influence on me and Fellini has always been an inspiration.

DS   How have light and motion affected your interpretations of feeling?

JD   Light is a potent symbol and extremely important for creating mood. I use it as a metaphor for the spiritual. In *Bedroom Window with Fan* (#130), for example, light is as much an object as the fan and crystals. I also equate movement resulting in blurred motion with a sense of mystery as in *Maggie in Church* (#28).

DS   You repeatedly use diagonal shafts of light to reveal aspects of a face or form. Are you conscious of using this visual convention?

JD   If I see light when I'm photographing, I try to manipulate it. Light can be a magical element in a composition, like the light cutting across the neck of *Gwen* (#114). When I successfully make light tangible and visible, I think it is graphically beautiful. My favorite time to photograph is late afternoon, because of a glowing quality to the light, especially against a dark sky. In *Self-portrait, Craters of the Moon* (#6), the shadows are long and everything is washed by the glowing sun. I look anonymous because my body reflects the light, is completely white, and devoid of detail. In *Stefania* (#29) I created a single source of light with a slide projector. She held a globe that functioned like a prism.

DS   Are you also interested in mirrors as a way of tampering with light?

JD   Yes, mirrors, glass of all types, water, anything reflective. Luminosity and reflection imply the mysterious – something that is felt but not known intellectually. I want my photographs to search for knowledge that is beyond fact. I use mirrors, water, light, glass that you cannot really see through as metaphors for puzzling, unanswerable questions.

DS   When did you start making self-portraits?

JD   I have some that date from 1963.

DS   Were they class assignments or personal artistic choices?

JD   I did them for myself. They satisfied some basic curiosity and provided a way to get at strong emotional imagery. In *Self-portrait* (#2) from 1965, I obscured my identity and made myself look extremely unattractive by pushing my face against the glass to distort my features. I remember choosing this piece of glass, because the splattered paint on the surface reminded me of stars, planets, or nebula in the universe. I was relating the universe of the stars with the universe of the mind. I was born on June 21st, the summer solstice and the longest day of the year. I have always felt a profound connection to the seasons and the cosmic, a theme that repeatedly appears in my work.

DS   Do self-portraits disclose more detailed information about an artist's feelings than other kinds of photography?

JD   Absolutely. Alfred Steiglitz did his equivalents and Paul Caponigro and Minor White created sequences of photographs to personify their inner feelings and emotional states. But when an artist places herself in front of a camera, it's extremely direct. It's hard to miss the point, which is one of the reasons I photographed other people first. I started doing photographs of other women, who were close to my age and usually in the arts, as stand-ins for myself. By selecting the right surrogates, I was able

to convey some of my feelings. I don't like to disclose everything at once. I try to achieve a balance between how much I reveal and how much I hold back. *Twinka Thiebaud, actress, model* (#20) with the see-through dress is a perfect example of this principle. Her sheer dress with the floral pattern and bows is infinitely more seductive than if she were photographed nude, even if she was in the same position and had the same expression on her face. Twinka looks extremely frightened, which may have related to my own fear of the unknown. There are numerous yin-yang aspects to my work: death and light, control and letting go, revealing and concealing, disclosure and revelation.

DS   Do you use the self-portrait as a means of fixing identity?

JD   It's like self-analysis. When you photograph yourself, you have in mind one thing and after reviewing the proofs may be surprised to see you've uncovered something else. In any case, I'm not trying to make a picture that's going to pin me down. The process is more exploratory. If I take risks the experience will unconsciously lead me to discover something new. I would hope some of the work had a universal, timeless quality and might help a viewer to recognize aspects of him or herself.

DS   Are you continually self-creating during the process of scrutinizing yourself?

JD   The creative process has something to do with production and reproduction, life and growth, evolution. That's why it's boring and horrible to repeat oneself. Discovery and change are essential.

DS   How does the concept of performance relate to narrative aspects of your image-making?

JD   I think of individual portraits as short stories. The expressions on the model's face, the pose, clothes or costume, all play a part in the construction of the narrative. When I photograph someone, I like being in control. After arranging the props and composition, my job is to get my subjects to willingly perform. In the self-portraits, I'm the actress, director, and photographer. The self-portraits in the landscape felt like ritualistic performances or earthworks.

DS   Why did you move away from the exploitable other onto the vulnerable self?

JD   I knew I could never ask a model to look ridiculous or be exposed to danger. It was essential for me to be free to experiment and express myself or the pictures would never have achieved their strength of vision and power.

DS   Did you plan to make self-portraits in the landscape, or did they evolve from your travels?

JD   Initially, I thought I would photograph the landscape because I had been making portraits for about fifteen years and I wanted a change. I started constructing ritualistic compositions, putting candles in the landscape and even found a few willing models in the desert who posed nude for me. In *Man with Horse's Skull* (#78), a nude guy wearing a mask-like horse's skull stands theatrically in front of a huge landscape backdrop or stage set. It was an attempt to make a mythical centaur figure – part horse, part man. I shot this picture in Nevada, where I found the skull. I took a few pictures with other people, but ultimately decided to use myself. *My Hands, Death Valley* (#1) was the first picture in the self-portraits in the landscape series. One day, waiting in my car for my traveling companion, Gail Skoff, I realized I was staring at the landscape through the car window. There was a green cast to the glass and it changed my perception of the land. I decided to photograph my hands on the car window, as if I was removing cataracts, metaphorically pulling the glass away to see the landscape more clearly. I had been taking pictures in the landscape for about a year when I did this self-portrait. After reviewing all my contact sheets, that image stood out as the most important picture I had taken in a long time. I finally realized I had to photograph myself, using the Western landscape as a background – not the grand, beautiful scenery of William Henry Jackson, Carleton Watkins or Albert Bierstadt, but a stark, more primeval view.

DS   Is that why you chose to photograph in black and white?

JD   Yes. I began using both color and black and white, but color was a distraction. Black and white seemed so much stronger and more like dried bones. I only work in color when the subject matter demands it.

DS   Were all the self-portraits in the landscape shot with a 4 x 5?

JD   Yes. For most I used a wide-angle 90 mm lens, which I hadn't used for a long time and haven't used since. A built-in timer gave me about ten seconds to run out in front of the camera. Once in a while, I would have Gail Skoff snap the shutter for me, but only if I posed myself farther away than a ten-second run. I methodically rehearsed each shot, marking my place with a twig or pebble, so I wouldn't have to think about it when the camera was activated. Occasionally, I wouldn't arrive at my position in time and blurry movement would result. I never knew exactly how I was going to appear and I found the chance aspect in the composition process liberating. Similarly, in my early portraits I composed the model and environment carefully, but for years, the moment I snapped the shutter, I would unconsciously look away or look down. Once I realized I did that, I tried to force myself to look, but ultimately felt it was an intrusion. I didn't want to make the models nervous or self-conscious.

DS   How many trips did you make during the course of this series of self-portraits in the landscape?

JD   I'm not exactly sure, probably ten. I started the series in 1980 and I did the last photographs in 1983. The trips usually lasted ten days to two weeks. I travelled with Gail Skoff on the longer, more ambitious trips, but I went with other photographers for shorter periods. I returned to the Badlands of South Dakota three times, but didn't retrace my steps, exploring unfamiliar sections of that particular national park each time. I had been to Craters of the Moon once many years before and had visited Yellowstone as a child. Most of the other trips were to discover new surroundings.

DS   How important was Georgia O'Keefe's work in formulating your images of the Southwest?

JD   I met her once for about thirty seconds at Ansel Adams' house in California and was thrilled to see her. I never saw her when I was in New Mexico, although I tried. I was struggling with my identity and kept thinking about what it meant to be a woman artist in New Mexico where Georgia O'Keefe was the classic prototype. Some of the symbolic imagery in her paintings of the Southwest initially influenced my photography – the bones, antlers, the barren black hills, but I couldn't make her iconography my own. I ended up rejecting most of my efforts.

DS   What role does religion have in your iconographic interpretations, particularly in relation to the landscape?

JD   I never thought about religion in relation to the landscape. If anything, I was concerned with ritual. While living in the Southwest, I attended a number of Indian dances and ceremonies. Those elaborate performances with costumes and props, many of which relate to the land and seasons, reverberated inside me, although I never tried to imitate them. I wanted my compositions to be dramatic. The placement of the small human against the vast natural landscape, which I viewed as a magnificent scenic backdrop or monumental stage set, is a recurring theme. A number of examples have an element of chance and potential danger. I performed personal rituals, consciously putting myself in risky situations. For example, in *Self-portrait with Sparkler* (#14), I stood on the edge of a geyser hole full of boiling water in Yellowstone, and I walked across jagged volcanic rocks in my bare feet; in *Self-portrait in Grasslands* (#8), I walked through the tall grasses in the Badlands of South Dakota, where I knew there were rattlesnakes. I was terrified of accidentally stepping on one, because I couldn't see where I was going.

DS   Was it exciting?

JD   Yes, and scary. I thought I was crazy and couldn't figure out why I felt compelled to do these things. It was a test of my nerve, a kind of physical experiment, the way men put themselves in jeopardy by climbing mountains or fighting wars to demonstrate their manliness. On some level, I was proving my self-reliance. Most people would never dream of doing some of the things I did, like taking my clothes off in public. Even though the sites were very remote, there was always a chance somebody would come along.

DS   Were you ever caught?

JD   Once at Zabriski Point in Death Valley. I decided I had to photograph myself lying on a bench. I calculated a new car arrived at this spot about every thirty seconds, but I thought I could whip off my clothes, take the picture and get dressed again in the allotted time. I miscalculated and some people walked down and saw me lying on the bench. They looked at me and giggled; they were more embarrassed than I was. Another time, at the Craters of the Moon, I was totally unaware people were watching. I had set up the shot near the parking lot and was working fast because the sun was about to go down. As I walked back to the camera and started putting my clothes on, I noticed a car had parked down the hill, waiting for me to finish before entering the lot. As soon as I dressed, a couple drove up and parked, smiling at me as they walked up the hill. The only time it was remotely scary was when I photographed *Self-portrait with Petroglyph* (#15) in New Mexico. I don't know if I was actually on an Indian reservation, but it was private land, and the Indians consider the petroglyphs sacred. I knew I was trespassing, but the picture was irresistible. The snake looks sperm-like, as if it's entering me and it also looks like an umbilical cord, as if I'm giving birth. I don't know what interpretation the Indians would give it. I used it for my own metaphorical meanderings. After I took the photograph, I dressed and started to walk to where Linda Connor, my traveling companion on that trip, was photographing some petroglyphs. I looked down the hill and noticed a man standing across the road stark naked, his pants down around his ankles, looking at me. I really got scared. I casually walked over to Linda and said, "Don't say anything, but look across the street. There's a nude man standing on the edge of the road." We both decided to ignore him. When he saw I wasn't alone, he disappeared. We were in the middle of nowhere and I don't know where he came from or where he went.

DS   Is photographing yourself more controlled and pre-planned than photographing others?

JD   The self-portraits in the landscape have a specific look. In that sense, they were pre-planned. But I never knew precisely what I would do once I got to a site. I often took props with me, but they didn't always work. In *Self-portrait with Mask* (#17) I am sitting in the dunes at White Sands wearing a mask I had recently purchased in Mexico during the Day of the Dead festivities. The mask has a strange, distorted male face. I delighted in combining a male face with a woman's body, a shocking androgynous figure, which I find mythical. I had not planned for my dog to run over and start digging a hole between my legs while I was waiting for the timer to go off, which added another surprising and humorous element to the composition. Though I had taken many other pictures that day, this is one of the few where my dog entered the frame. On one of the last trips, I took a length of white rope, although I had no idea how I would use it. It seemed like a strong visual element and I kept looking for ways to incorporate it in my pictures. If I hadn't taken the rope with me, I doubt if I would have found that white rock in the middle of an expanse of red earth, which I tied up in *Self-portrait with White Rock* (#12). It was an amazing natural object! God knows where it came from or why it was there. This sort of free association is typical of the way I think and work. In this picture, the rope was pre-planned, but the realization wasn't. My method is similar when photographing people. I recognize a person with a soulful face, but can never foretell what his house is like, what kind of props might be there, or what the light is going to be like. *John Gutmann* (#97) for example, has an interesting face and personality and I thought I could make a

good portrait of him, but I didn't know he collected skulls, shrunken heads, and Day of the Dead objects until I arrived at his house. Once I entered his domain, I found the idea of pairing him with these symbolic objects irresistible. In contrast, I think Annie Leibovitz has elaborate ideas about what she wants to do with people and then gets them to realize her fantasies, like Whoopi Goldberg in a bathtub full of milk or the Blues Brothers with blue faces.

DS   Do you find a great difference conceptually or artistically between *Self-portrait with Mist* (#7) 1980 and *Self-portrait Holding Up Rock* (#13) 1983?

JD   I wanted the earliest self-portraits in the landscape to be anonymous. I didn't want to show my face, so either I'm in silhouette, photographed from the back or I'm very far away from the camera. In *Golden Light and Wind* and *Self-portrait with Sparkler* (#14), my hair covers my face and my body is fairly dark. It's not easy to recognize me. The earlier pictures are subdued and motionless. I'm lying down, sitting or standing. I consider *Self-portrait with Mist* (#7) one of the most heroic pictures in the series. It's a romanticized vision of woman – strong, intrepid, courageous. The path that leads into the mist, which I've just passed through, symbolizes the unknown and is a metaphor for my own life. Midway through the series, I began to use makeup on my face, looked directly at the camera, and took more close-ups. I was much more willing to reveal myself physically. I photographed the last few images in the series, like *Self-portrait Holding up Rock* (#13) where I tried to create the illusion of superhuman feats of strength, after I moved back to California and had passed the mystery age of forty and survived. By 1983, I felt much stronger physically and mentally, and I wanted to show that in the pictures. I used my body more actively and dynamically in the landscape. After I photographed the last few, I knew the series was complete.

DS   Why has landscape photography been practiced primarily by men?

JD   Women started to work in nature only recently.

Pioneering photographers, like William Henry Jackson, had to be explorers because of the physical demands of travel. Women traditionally photographed people. Today, women can throw all their equipment into a car and drive into the wilderness. They don't have to use a mule and an 8 x 10 view camera.

DS   Were Lucy Lippard's critical writings an influence on your self-portraits in the landscape?

JD   I read her book, *Overlay: Contemporary Art and the Arts of Prehistory* (New York: Pantheon, 1983), while I was making the black and white self-portraits in the landscape and was fascinated by her ideas. It made me feel this work was part of a tradition.

DS   In your landscape self-portraits, were you investigating nineteenth-century assumptions identifying women and nature?

JD   I was pitting myself against nature, not trying to become one with it. I recognized the obvious symbols and would use them whenever it seemed appropriate. Sometimes it worked and sometimes it didn't.

DS   Were you reading about nineteenth-century America and the westward expansion?

JD   No, I wasn't thinking too much about the nineteenth century. I was thinking about the future, being on another planet. Part of the appeal of the Southwest was that it looks like the surface of a planet other than Earth. I love the contrast of soft, human flesh against the sharpness and hardness of the landscape. It was the perfect Spartan backdrop for my little dramas and fit the mood I was trying to produce with my images.

DS   Were you dealing with the concepts of *terra incognita*, or the unfamiliar territory versus *terra cognita*, the known earth?

JD   Not consciously. Being a stranger in a strange land was more exciting and mysterious than New Mexico, which eventually became too familiar. Once I moved to New Mexico, which has a beautiful and dramatic landscape, I took only one picture of myself I liked, *Self-portrait with Petroglyph* (#15). When I returned home to Santa Fe from my travels, I created color self-portraits in my living room, which evolved from mundane day after day activities – eating, cleaning, trying to stay in shape.

DS   Did you consciously try to make funny images when you started working on the color self-portraits in Santa Fe?

JD   I was at a low ebb personally and had cabin fever. I had been photographing in the landscape, but couldn't always travel and needed to work in or near my house. I preferred to continue the autobiographical themes I had been exploring in nature and it occurred to me that the creation of stereotypical personae – alter egos of myself – would be an interesting way of dealing with issues that were very real to me at the time. I built a theatrical stage set with a parted background curtain and pretended to be a character actress on stage. For *Spider Woman* (#62) I borrowed barbells from my neighbor, who lifted weights. I got dressed in the costume, held the barbells and knocked on my neighbor's door. She was surprised and found my persona hilarious. I knew the different characters were humorous and satiric. These photographs helped me get through a hard time. It helped to make fun of myself and the popular stereotypes of women's roles. Humor can break the tension. But they were also very serious. They are extensions of my earlier portraits of women in costume, a theme I've explored since the late 1960s. I willingly show a dark side of myself. In *Eating* (#65), I presented myself as the bored housewife sitting at home and gorging on food. I often felt like the maid in *Death by Ironing* (#64). I was home cooking and cleaning. It was a drag, but it was part of my life.

DS   What is the meaning of *Elephant Woman Steps Out* (#61)?

JD   It has to do with body image and feeling overweight. Almost every woman is obsessed with her weight at one time or another. The title was inspired by the movie "Elephant Man." I was punning on expressions like "fat as a pig," "big as an elephant." Wearing an old-fashioned girdle made me appear even fatter.

DS   Did you intend to produce such garish, merci-
less images?

JD   Of course. The color portraits were shot with a
large format camera to emphasize the various tex-
tures of satin, feathers, food, etc. Their palpable
sense of flesh was important.

DS   Did you want them to lack the seductiveness or
glamour for which your earlier portraits are known?

JD   It wasn't a matter of wanting, it was a matter of
not caring. When I lived in New Mexico, I felt anonymous and isolated. I didn't think anyone would see
my work and I was doing it to amuse myself. These
color self-portraits helped dissipate my anger at certain aspects of my life at that time.

DS   When you confronted the dilemmas of the
modern woman through the color self-portraits,
did it help you clarify your own identity and sense
of what you were trying to be?

JD   That has always been my primary goal. The
search is constant and the end is never clear-cut.
I went through a long period from about 1980
until 1985 when I examined myself very critically.
I showed some of my silliest, dopiest, fattest, most
ugly aspects. At a certain point, I didn't want to know
the inner workings of my mind anymore. Self-
absorption was too isolating. I put myself through
the ringer and became a stronger person. I had
learned everything I could stand to know about
myself to that point and wanted to go on.

DS   Do you consider these color self-portraits the
most feminist statements you've made?

JD   It depends one what brand of feminism you
believe in. I see them as very feminist, as well as personal and surreal.

DS   Were you active in the feminist movement in
San Francisco?

JD   I was certainly aware of it, interested, sympathetic; but I'm not an activist. I never marched in a
parade.

DS   How has writing affected your image making?

JD   I keep a diary of dreams. When I have a particularly good dream I write it down and later may build

on it for a photograph. For example, the color self-
portrait, *Scream* (#63), was based on a dream. *Teenage
Diary* (#71,72) is an early example, though not the
first, where I used writing. The so-called love letters
contain excerpts from letters I had written but never
sent. In *Love letters #3* (#73-75), the writing is actually a
list I made talking on the phone to a friend. *Fourth of
July, State #4* (#69) has words. More recently, I've been
writing a history of my relationships with men, and
taking excerpts from my writings and combining
them with computer-manipulated photographs.

DS   Were you able to create your own work during
the time you did the photographic memoir of
Imogen Cunningham?

JD   I didn't do anything else when I worked on that
book except photograph the people I interviewed,
but those pictures were in the service of the book,
and not really my personal work. I think my best
work is internally motivated. In terms of Imogen's
photographs, I was very familiar with her *oeuvre* and
felt a kinship with it.

DS   What about her words? Did you investigate her
writings? How did concentrating on another artist
affect your own vision?

JD   Yes, her writings were poignant, but only rein-
forced what I'd already known and felt about
Imogen. I remember a group of letters she received
from Morris Graves, an artist she had photographed
in the 1950s. She really admired him and wanted to
photograph him again. She plagued him for twenty
years and eventually got her picture. That tenacity I
always admired in her. One of the biggest surprises
in researching her archive was finding hundreds of
photographs she'd taken of her sons, when they were
young. They were the cutest photographs of children
I'd ever seen and caused me to seriously consider
having a child. This incredible legacy of her relationship to her kids was gorgeous and unexpectedly
touching. It was an aspect of her life I didn't know
and it uncovered a part of myself I didn't know.

DS   How did your two-year involvement with *Body
and Soul* affect your work?.

JD   I didn't do much of my personal photography then either, but I gained a lot working on that book, because the process suggested several new directions for my work. Previously, I tried to select the most expressive portrait of an individual. For *Body and Soul,* I took a lot of 35mm close-ups of a subject's face during the interviews, showing different expressions and aspects of their personality. It was impossible to pick one definitive portrait to summarize each woman. In the design of the book, we composed the headshots like a continuous film strip. Later, when I made the first couple of combined image tableaux, I used some of these pictures out of context. I paired expressive headshots with other imagery to create fictional narratives. I also exhibited some of the full-length portraits from *Body and Soul,* which stand on their own.

DS   Were any of your early photographs conceived as multiple image narratives?

JD   I always thought in terms of groups of pictures – women, men, myself. My first inclination to assemble several photographs into one piece was in 1976, when I did the *Arles Suite* (#131-137). Before the mid-1970s, I was interested in sequencing in the same way Minor White worked – a whole group would end up greater than individual parts. The triptych *Oracle* (#59), which I did in 1984, refers to the Delphic shrine, the unknown, and the cosmic, exemplified by the stars and moon, heaven and earth. I integrated biblical stories of the plagues – raining blood and fishes – and the serpent, who stands for knowledge as well as sexuality in the Garden of Eden. The faces represent the voices of the Oracle. I painted my face with the phases of the moon to correspond with the other cosmic references. The depiction of the full moon with blood on my forehead represents menstruation, which is cyclical, graphically illustrating the way women are physically tied to the moon, tides, and nature.

DS   What role does intuition have in your combined image tableaux?

JD   For some of the large-scale narratives I have a pre-conceived idea of the overriding theme, but most of the time, I start with a single image, aware it is loaded with meaning. Then I search through contact sheets for other images that, in combination, would produce a thought-provoking story. It's an intuitive process. A perfect example is *End of Innocence* (#49). The photographs were all taken within a month or so. The photographs on the upper left of snakes and upper right of a bird were both taken at the Museum of Natural History in New York on the same day. I used to walk around the Museum looking for objects I felt had symbolic meaning. I just knew there was something about the snake that was scary and ominous, biblical and sexual; I figured I'd be able to use it, but I had no idea how. I never thought of the snake picture as a singular image. And the same is true with the picture of the dark bird in flight, which represented the idea of release, freedom, and escape, the essence of the phoenix. It was wintertime and a few days later as I walked through Central Park, I noticed the empty branches of trees were loaded with birds. So I took some pictures of them. Afterwards, a bird-shaped cloud and a wing-shaped cloud appeared in the sky over the bare trees. It seemed like an amazing coincidence, so I took those pictures. The same week I visited a friend, where I saw the beautiful picture of the water bird with a fish in its mouth, which I thought suggested the essence of pursuit and capture. I also took a picture of my friend pulling a black stocking onto her foot, which I shaped to look like a snake, adding an erotic note to the storyline. I had all these pictures on various contact sheets, and started arranging them to see what made sense in a visual, symbolic, and graphic or structural way. *End of Innocence* (#49) also includes more personal references, because my friend felt trapped and wanted to escape a bad relationship. While empathizing with her plight, I used her experience as a way of talking about my own frustrations. So it wasn't specifically about me or her, but through my friend's situation, I created a narrative that talked about all of those ideas.

DS Had you completed several narratives using a multipanel format by then?

JD Yes. I started doing the multiples at the end of 1987 and that one came about two years later. I was gathering photographs, which I thought of as raw material. I didn't always have an exact, set narrative in mind when I was making the multipanel pieces, although all of them are fictional. For the later ones, when I was spending a lot of time photographing at the Natural History Museum, the theme of cosmic evolution, the way everything in nature and civilization is connected, one thing to another, became my central focus.

DS Are your memory pieces dreams or nightmares?

JD Probably some of both. They're waking daydreams in the form of a nightmare. *Memory #1* (#43) came about by accident. I did some photographs of a friend giving birth to her child and at the same time shot intense expressions on her face to use separately. At one point, I also shot some pictures of a guy holding his carving knife. Nothing was violent or menacing about either situation but together I realized I could create a whole story about potential violence, violence to women, and the relationship between sex, pleasure, and pain. There's a lot of ambiguity in the woman's expression about whether she's ecstatic and having an orgasm or if she's in pain. *Memory #2* (#44) interweaves headshots of Geraldine Fitzgerald with mountains and an empty teacup. This renowned actress has a very expressive face, strong and craggy. Her seemingly fearful and sad expressions are juxtaposed with the empty teacup, to suggest loneliness and the passage of time. I equate the cragginess of her skin with the bleak frozen land of the mountain ranges, which for me signifies death. Obviously, this is not a story about Geraldine Fitzgerald. It's a story about aging. *Memory #4* (#45) was based on an incestuous experience a friend had as a child. My friend's painful story affected me deeply. In the top two images, a little three-year-old girl is playing happily and smiling,

but the water squirting up between her legs has sexual overtones, even though there is a real sense of innocence to the image. The center bottom panel shows her running away and crying, as though something frightening occurred. The two photographs of intertwined branches suggest the tangled web in which the child is caught or lost. The man could be the culprit, or a concerned parent. His role is ambiguous. These photographs were taken randomly. There is no relationship between the man, whom I photographed in France, to the children, who live in New Jersey, or the North Carolina landscape, but when I put them together, an implied meaning or story results. *Playing with Fire* (#48) is the only self-portrait in this series. When I was living in New York I often felt miserable and tortured. I think this piece has a gothic feeling to it that reminds me of Joan of Arc. In the bottom image I'm holding a fireplace poker in front of my face but it looks like I'm branded. Also, there is a suggestion of violence, being burned or hurt and in pain.

DS You used to photograph provocative subjects. Is your current goal the creation of provocative narratives?

JD Definitely. By juxtaposing unlikely photographs it is possible to create a more exciting and shocking tale. However, I don't think the more recent Polaroid tableaux are disturbing, which somehow follows the pattern and path of my internal life. Like many artists, I create different things based on what's going on in my life. Some artists, like Francis Bacon, are tortured throughout their life. His paintings are strong and powerful, but there's hardly one that isn't agonized. I've gone in and out of times when I'm more placid. Right now, my work is full of humor.

DS How political are your implicit narratives?

JD Some of my pictures are extremely political from a feminist perspective. The early series of portraits are political by virtue of the new way I portrayed women as independent, strong yet fearsome, unafraid of their own sexuality. *Woman with Bomb* (#144,145) and *Fourth of July, State #4* (#69) are overtly political. The double self-portrait *He Won't Be the First Adulterer President* (#147,148) is political and satirical. There's something pitifully ludicrous about men like Gary Hart and Jimmy Swaggert being caught and then forced to be publicly remorseful.

DS How have living and working in environments different from San Francisco, where you spent most of your adult life, caused you to explore new directions?

JD The places I've lived have always influenced and advanced my work. Living in New York transformed my photography. When I moved there in January 1987, it was too cumbersome and difficult to walk around the city with a 4 x 5 camera. I finally decided it was better to take pictures than not, even if I got a grainy negative. So I started using a 35mm camera, which really freed me. After a while I discovered if I printed a negative out of focus, I could eliminate the grain. Consequently, many of the multiple panel pieces are printed out of focus, but also because I preferred to make them more generic, suppressing detail to achieve the essence of an idea.

DS What impact did not having a stable home and darkroom have on your creative endeavors?

JD I think it had an enormous impact. I moved twelve times from January 1987 through May 1991 – at least ten times in the first two and a half years. One apartment I lived in for two months had a darkroom, but the first time I used it there was a fire. The only other darkroom I had was in the basement of my last New York apartment, which was a terrible dungeon. For the first couple of years I accumulated my negatives and travelled back and forth between New York and California to my San Anselmo darkroom. I printed all the large black and white combined image tableaux in California while I was living in New York. I began to hate the darkroom. *The City* (#46) was a direct response to my fractured existence in New York City and involves the idea of anonymity, being lost or trampled in a crowd. The impenetrable, helmeted faces of the statues are frightening and look like bondage masks. After I adjusted to living in New York, I became more internal, which I think happens to a lot of people when they live there. I started writing. When I rented out my California house, I began to investigate ways of making art without a darkroom, which led me to computers. Now I am back in California and have the best darkroom I've ever had, as well as my computer.

DS Were the color narrative tableaux the first time you worked with the large format Polaroid camera?

JD Yes. Shortly after Polaroid started the program they invited me to participate, but I wasn't sure what I wanted to do and for years kept putting it off. Finally, somebody told me Polaroid was going to stop the program so I immediately scheduled a time. I preferred working with the same problems I confronted in the black and white multiple panels, but until about a week before my appointment, hadn't figured out a way to transfer my previous working method to a room-sized camera and thought I would have to do one of my portraits. Suddenly, I realized I could take advantage of the color potential of the camera, by making still life collages combining color materials from various sources and my own black and white photographs, which I ultimately photographed with the Polaroid. I really loved working that way and wanted to continue beyond the two days of my grant, but I didn't have enough new images to make it worthwhile. The Polaroid pieces were done after I had settled down in New York City; they're much quieter, less tortured and more philosophical than the black and white multiple panel pieces. *Cycles* (#50-52) the large nine-panel piece is related to *End of Innocence* (#49) and has a cosmic orientation. The source material came almost exclusively from the Museum of Natural History in New York. In it I chronicled the evolution of culture, starting with ancient civilization on the bottom row, represented by a mask, the mystery of science in the center, and the book on the left, which happens to be a Koran, but which could have been the Bible or any other learned book. To me the book symbolizes knowledge. The center panel contains the elements, crystalline and marbleized objects, which represent earth. The top row is about the universe; on the far left is a picture of a galaxy; the middle section shows a bird taking flight, leaving earth; the harp represents celestial music, the music of the spheres. *Blue Angel* (#53) is more ambiguous and enigmatic. The main theme is love exemplified by the couple in the center. *The Pond* (#54, 55) combines eroticism and a search for inner truth. In the top panel, a Japanese man is tattooing a woman's back; the monk-like figure walking on water in the center suggests religion; the fishes on the bottom imply sperm and the continuation of life.

DS   How important are the titles of your work?

JD   It varies. They distinguish one picture from another as in the series of black and white self-portraits. Often they contribute clues to what the pictures are about. Sometimes the titles come easily, for example, all the color self-portraits seemed to name themselves. When the ideas behind the pictures get more complex, as in the narrative tableaux, the titles are more important, for they purposefully add another layer of information and provocativeness.

DS   Considering the body of your work, what have you garnered from your early experiences growing up in Hollywood?

JD   Among my earliest memories are weekly visits to my father's movie theatre. I regularly accompanied him on expeditions to buy advertising posters, candy, and other supplies for the theatre. I spent many hours playing games in the darkened theatre and cataloging glossy pictures of young starlets. When I was a teenager, I worked as an usher, popcorn and candy seller, and cashier. On my break I would see the same ten-minute excerpt from the current feature. All this had a huge impact on me, my becoming a photographer, and ultimately on my work. For a while I thought about becoming an actress, but I didn't have the inclination to pursue it. I had teenage fantasies about being a glamourous star and even made up a good 1940s Hollywood movie star name for myself – Gina Lester. I took

filmmaking at school and I made a few short films, but the prospect of working with other people seemed too complex. I preferred the meditative act of photographing, something I could do by myself. I became a photographer because that's what I wanted to do more than anything else in the world.

This dialogue took place in Palo Alto, California during January 1992.

Donna Stein *is an art historian, independent critic and curator, who has written widely on nineteenth-century and contemporary photography.*

Dissonance *A Dissertation on the work of Judy Dater*

Michiko Kasahara

Dissonance. One of the main reasons Judy Dater's work touches such a chord in modern women is the dissonance that flows endlessly through it. Her pictures express something deeper than mere surface sentimentalism. They express the feelings of loneliness and unease shared by many socially aware, modern women. While women have made progress toward throwing off the subordinate position traditionally considered their role, and are better able to face others on equal terms, they still live with feelings of loneliness and unease. (This is not, of course, to say that they necessarily feel tragic or despairing.) However, refusing to be confined within society's conception of "womanhood," modern women have found themselves in unavoidable conflict with their own, inner conception.

Dissonance. It is the confrontation of self. We must realize that only through confrontation with one's self may we achieve a mature and sympathetic relationship with others. And this confrontation takes place not only on a personal level, but on social, historical, and political levels as well. If we do not understand ourselves, it is impossible to understand or sympathize with others. However, we cannot escape from discord within ourselves, or in our relationships with others, and it is this discord that leads to loneliness and unease.

Dissonance. "Revelation, confrontation and empathy are the dominant qualities of Dater's work" (James L. Enyeart); ". . . coldly objective and spontaneously subjective" (Joan Murray).[1] These descriptions of Judy Dater's work have a common base, as does the depth of our feelings toward self, others, or society – all these responses are the product of feelings of loneliness and unease.

Dissonance. Is there a cure for the loneliness and unease borne by modern women? Can these feelings be diminished through relationships with other people, through traditional roles of daughter, wife or lover, through the experience of years, through creative work, career or hobbies? Is it possible to lessen and finally eliminate these feelings?

Judy Dater's photographs work towards this end and have a brilliance all their own. In our present time, when expression of women's sensibility represents a large movement not only in the field of photography, but in society as a whole, the importance of her work cannot be overstated. Judy Dater is a true innovator, facing her loneliness and unease and creating her pictures in a state of dissonance.

The content of Judy Dater's work, rather than its chronology or stylistic evolution, is the primary concern of this essay – content rooted in social and historical background, and filled with a resonant dissonance.

She was born in Hollywood in 1941. Her father managed a cinema and it is easy to imagine the influence this must have had on her both visually and emotionally.

Judy Dater was stimulated both consciously and unconsciously by the feminism and counterculture movements of the 1960s and 1970s, and is one of the new breed of liberated women. In 1963, Betty Friedan's *The Feminine Mystique* was published, and presented the backbone philosophy of the second women's liberation movement. Riding on the crest of the student power movement that was rocking world capitals, the so-called "Women's Lib" movement was formed around the "Betrayed Feminine Socialists."[2] Feminist art is said to have started with the publication of Judy Chicago's *Dinner Party* (1974-1980) and Kate Millett's *Sexual Politics* (1970). In photography, too, women were quick to catch on to this trend. In 1975, Anne Tucker published a book entitled *The Woman's Eye,* in which she combined the work of ten women photographers with her own essays.

It is significant that the cover of *The Woman's Eye* is a portrait taken by Judy Dater. The photograph shows a famous model named *Twinka* (#20), sitting at the base of a redwood tree, one long, bony hand on the bark, the other clutching her knee. She wears a thin dress embroidered with flowers, and sunlight streams through it to clearly reveal the outline of her slim body, as her eyes remain firmly fixed on the camera.

The Woman's Eye attempted to reassess the work of pioneer women photographers and to deepen the understanding of individual women's sensibilities. In comparing Judy Dater and Bea Nettles to the great woman photographers of the past – Kasebier, Benjamin Johnston, Bourke-White, Lange, Abbott, Morgan, Arbus and Wells – Anne Tucker said, "Although they share many of the same concerns and confront many of the same barriers, Dater and Nettles have not been discussed with the other photographers, mainly because too much has changed within photography and our culture for a direct comparison of the generations born before and after 1940."[3] "Too much has changed" – women have begun to find their own viewpoint.

In the course of growing up – in the home, at school, in the workplace, in the media and through everyday customs, we are subjected to a constant barrage of preconceptions about what makes a woman, what her position in society should be, and how she is expected to behave. Men have ruled society for so long that their view of the world has become the accepted one. In order to come up with a uniquely feminine viewpoint, women have had to look inside themselves, discover the masculine viewpoint that has been forced upon them since childhood, and remove those parts that they feel are not in keeping with their personal views. Women are finally beginning to awaken to their true selves and are forming a new perception of "woman," both physical and intellectual. They are challenging the accepted male image of woman, and this challenge is a revolutionary development.

There has been another important change as well. In the past, women photographers were accepted for their work despite their sex. Today, Judy Dater and other modern women photographers have the support of a large percentage of women and men who share their views – a support that is indicative of a new movement in society.

It was no coincidence that Judy Dater's pictures in *The Woman's Eye* were portraits – a genre she has explored from the beginning of her career right up to the present. In her four published books to date, portraits have accounted for a large percentage of the pictures.

In 1975, together with her mentor and husband, Jack Welpott, she produced a collection of photographs of modern, urban women entitled *Women and Other Visions.* (This book is particularly interesting in that it gives the viewer the opportunity to compare different approaches made by Dater and Welpott to the same subjects, and it illustrates the disparity between male and female viewpoints).

Imogen Cunningham: A Portrait (1979) is a collection of photographs by the legendary artist Imogen Cunningham, whom Judy Dater met while still a university student. Ms. Cunningham was eighty at the time. The two remained close friends until Ms. Cunningham's death at the age of ninety-three. In the book, Dater included interviews with Cunningham's friends and relatives, as well as her own outstanding portraits of them. The book brings the artist to life and beautifully reveals her.

In 1986, *Judy Dater: Twenty Years* was published, a retrospective of work produced during the first twenty years of her career. Nineteen eighty-eight marked the publication of *Body & Soul: Ten American Women,* the life stories of women from different walks of life, with photographs by Dater and interviews by Carolyn Coman.

Few of Judy Dater's portraits involve studio settings. Instead, she photographs her subjects in everyday surroundings. She includes furniture, wallpaper, pictures, or ornaments that the subjects may have selected themselves. The models wear clothes of their own choice and pose in their own environments. Despite the fact that her portraits are set in the most private surroundings, there is nothing domestic about them.

She usually places her subjects in the middle of the frame, and using a 4 x 5 sheet film camera, includes just enough of their surroundings to indicate their interests and tastes. The models, whether dressed in everyday clothes or nude, present their real faces to the camera, eyes focused beyond the lens on Ms. Dater, and ultimately, through her, on us the viewers. There is an implicit trust apparent in the portraits; subjects have relaxed enough to let Judy Dater capture their true appearance. Models are photographed in ordinary, everyday situations, and their expressions are not filled with joy, sorrow, or other strong emotions. At the same time, however, there is always an atmosphere of tension in her work, an electrical charge running between the subject and the photographer.

Judy Dater's portraits are portraits of the inner being more than the outer form with which photographic portraiture has traditionally been concerned. In her nude portraits, she does not aim to show the sheen of young skin, or to create beautiful, abstract shapes out of the female body. She shows the sags and wrinkles as they really are, concentrating, instead, on the personality and internal beauty of the subject.

In the field of photography, there are many more nude portraits of women than of men. Men have spent years experimenting with producing the ideal nude, and for the most part, have found it easier to work with women than with their own sex. However, the image of the ideal man is just as strong in the collective consciousness as that of the ideal woman. In the same way that a set idea of beauty is defined for women, men are expected to be strong, muscular, and masculine. When Dater takes a portrait of a male nude, however, it is merely the picture of a man who happens to have just removed his clothes. She shows him as he is, wrinkles and fat and all, without

ostentation or humiliation, just a normal body, like that which we all possess.

Dater's eye captures the figure, environment and expression of modern people and responds to the ambivalence, the discord, the dismay, the self-consciousness – *the dissonance.* She shows the inner side of the man or woman *as it is,* encompassing pleasantness and confidence, as well as the attendant unease.

In an interview about her self-portraits, Judy Dater said, "It's like writing in my diary when things are rough, or when there is some major event happening. I have that tendency with the self-portraits as well. When you have no other recourse you just have to stop and really look at yourself."[4]

Judy Dater has been involved in producing self-portraits since the 1960s. In 1982, soon after turning forty, she produced her most famous pictures in this genre: black and white nude self-portraits in nature. This series contrasts with the color self-portraits which depict various female roles thrust upon women by society.

In Dater's self-portraits, she delves deeper into her inner being than in her photographs of other people. It seems apparent that she decided to use her own body in order to focus more strongly on the loneliness, unease, and discord lurking within her. She shows the aging of her body and deals directly with her sexuality. Consider some of the images from this period: she appears naked on a solitary road in the desert, one hand covering her breasts while the other is over her groin, a look of fear on her face while she stands motionless *Self-portrait on Deserted Road* (#18); she stands naked on a rough rock in a lake, her hands behind her, legs spread, with the light of a sparkler bursting from between her thighs *Self-portrait with Sparkler* (#37); she lies in a fetal position across a barren, rocky landscape *Self-portrait with Stone* (#11).

She competes with the wildness of nature. She refuses to become a metaphor for nature, to harmonize with it, or to create an abstract beauty. In order to discover herself, to uncover her loneliness and unease, to open herself to relating and sympathizing with others in society, she challenges both nature and herself. She uses her own forty-year-old body aggressively, and rejects attempts at idealism or glorification.

In the color self-portraits shot in the studio, she dresses up to create a parody of the role-play that society forces upon women. She makes a joke of the way in which modern women, herself included, feel that they are bound to conform to these preconceived ideas. In one picture she stands attired in pink tank top, miniskirt, and servant's bonnet, arms filled with brush, duster, dustpan, iron, detergent and plastic wrap, a look of resignation on her heavily made-up face *Ms.Clingfree*. In another, she portrays a housewife wearing sexy lingerie and a silver-blond wig, sitting in the corner of the kitchen eating cake and strawberries *Eating* (#65). In another she has a bird cage on her head and is screaming into the camera *Scream* (#63). In yet another, wearing a mask, with breasts exposed, she depicts the queen of the night *Queen of the Night* (#60). She uses this kind of deformed role-play to show how women, herself included, have been taught to think of themselves, and the conflict and suffering this self-image involves. What she exposes encourages others to mistrust their preconceptions.

She has also experimented with landscapes, still life, computer-manipulated images, graphics, multiple exposures and multiple frames to express more directly her interior dissonance. Consider the picture of a dead deer floating on water *Dead Deer In Pond* (#31). A still life photograph shows perfume spray, a china book, and a lamp in the shape of the Virgin Mary atop a mirrored tray, two pictures of children beside it *Prayer* (#39). *Stairs, Mexico* (#129) consists of a round hole in a cracked wall and staircase.

In her more recent work, she has made close-ups of highly emotional faces and has combined images, some of them abstract, to create very large narrative pieces. Although she took many of the pictures with a sheet film camera, which is capable of showing the most minute detail, she has purposely blurred the enlarged prints in order to stress anonymity. The mood or feeling of the entire piece is of more interest than the individual or object she has photographed. For instance, her work entitled *Memory #1* (#43) consists of six images arranged vertically in two groups. There are three close-ups of a woman's face contorted in either ecstasy or sorrow, combined alternately with three pictures of the body and hands of a man holding a knife. It is like a scene from a nightmare, and like a nightmare half-forgotten, it has the power to move us, even though the details of the man's face and the situation itself have been lost. It is not the record of a particular person or incident. It is an expression of Judy Dater's subconscious dissonance, and it encompasses anger, joy, guilt, sympathy, shame, and self-indulgence.

Having long studied herself, Judy Dater can create work that contains both vibrant tension and a deep, quiet gentleness. She bears her loneliness and unease and allows herself no compromise as she struggles to answer unanswerable questions. In doing so, she leads us to places women have not ventured before.

Michiko Kasahara *is a curator at the Tokyo Metropolitan Museum of Photography, Tokyo, Japan. Translated by Gavin Frew.*

Notes:
1. James L. Enyeart, *Judy Dater: Twenty Years* (Tucson: University of Arizona Press, 1988), xi.
2. Chizuko Ueno, *Kafuchosei to Shihonsei Marukusu Shugi Feminizumu no Chihei "The Patriarchal System and Capitalism: Horizons of Marxian Feminism."* (Iwanami Shoten, 1990), p.4.
3. Anne Tucker, "Introduction," *The Woman's Eye* (New York: Alfred A. Knopf, 1976), p.10.
4. Jeff Dunas, "The Interview," *Darkroom Photography Magazine* (October 1989), p.71.

Additional Photographs

101

102

103

104

105

101. Lovers #1,1964
102. Lovers #2,1964
103. Embrace,1965
104. Legion of Honor,1966
105. At Napoleon's tomb, Paris,1967

106

107

108

109

110

106. Aspen,1969
107. Joyce Goldstein,1969
108. Maria Moreno,1971
109. Gael and Rachel,1971
110. Maria and Legend,1971

113

111

112

111. Afternoon in Danville,1971

112. Danville bedroom,1971

113. Woman in white,
     Bloomington, Indiana,1971

114. Gwen,1972

115. Kathleen Kelly,1972

114

115

116

117

118

119

120

116. Valerie,1972

117. Cheri,1972

118. Maureen in mirror,1972

119. Fantasy in black and white,1973

120. Imogen in the mirror,1973

121

122

123

124

125

121. Daydreams, 1973

122. Laura Mae, 1973

123. Wally and Nadine, 1973

124. Bedroom, Arles, France, 1973

125. Kelly and Sybil, 1974

126

127

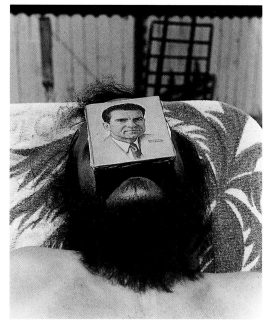

128

129

130

126. Maria Theresa,1974

127. Sandy,1975

128. Repose of the deposed,1975

129. Stairs, Mexico,1976

130. Bedroom window with fan,1977

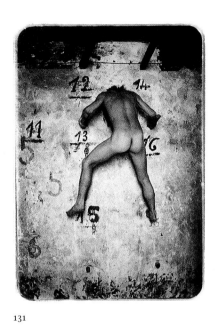

131, 132, 133, 134. Arles Suite, 1976-78

138. Patrick Nagatani, 1978
139. Hide, 1978

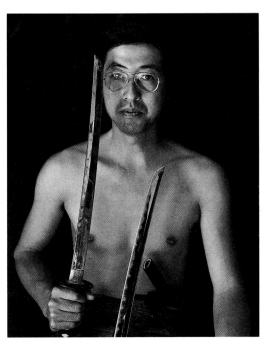

138

139

135

137

136

135, 136, 137. Arles Suite, 1976-1978

140. Bernie,1978
141. Salah Jahine, Cairo,1980

140

141

243

142

144

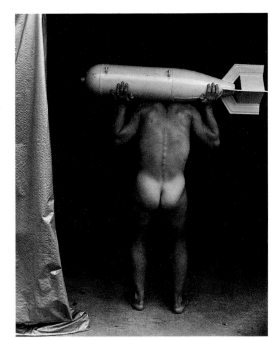

145

143

146

142. Man with bird, Pittsburgh,1981
143. Gail with rain,1982
144. Women with bomb #4,1984
145. Women with bomb #2,1984
146. Waterfall, North Carolina,1985

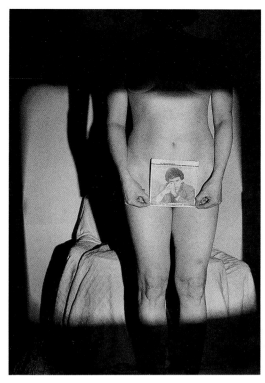

147

148

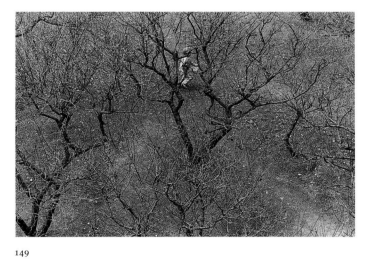

149

150

147. He won't be "first adulterer" president #1,1988
148. He won't be "first adulterer" president #2,1988
149. In the brambles, Japan,1991
150. Honeymoon,1991

245

Personal History

1941
I was born in Hollywood, California on June 21, the summer solstice. I am an only child. I grew up in Los Angeles, a tomboy and movie fanatic. The fact my father owned a movie theater made me somewhat popular with the other kids. I spent a lot of time playing in the darkened theater – an experience that probably influenced my desire to become a photographer and spend so many hours in a darkroom. I went to junior high and high school in Los Angeles. My favorite classes were always the art classes. I worked on the yearbook, drawing cartoons.

1959
I graduated from Fairfax High School and entered the University of California, Los Angeles as an art education major. I was not very interested in becoming a teacher, but at that time, it was something young women were encouraged to do as a safety net. I did not do very well my first two years at UCLA. I was not enrolled in a single art studio course until my third year. Once I got into the art classes, things started to improve.

1962-1963
I moved north, transferred from UCLA to San Francisco State University, and took my first photography course. I received my B.A. from San Francisco State University. I continued my graduate studies at San Francisco State towards an M.A. in art with an emphasis in photography. I had found the medium that allowed me to express the inexpressible.

1964
I received my teaching credentials and taught at Marina Junior High School in San Francisco for one semester, while continuing as a graduate student. I did not enjoy teaching junior high school, and after one semester chose to work at odd jobs in the photography field. I met Imogen Cunningham at a conference on the life and work of Edward Weston, held at Big Sur Hot Springs. Many other important photographers attended this event: Ansel Adams, Brett Weston, Cole Weston, Wynn Bullock, Peter Stackpole. Imogen stood out for me because she was so outrageous and irreverent. I was mesmerized by this eighty-year-old woman with incredible energy, funny clothes, a quick wit and acid tongue. She took some photographs of me and a few weeks later I went to see her at her home in San Francisco. We became friends,

and her work and approach to life became a lasting source of inspiration.

1968-1971
I began a collaborative project with Jack Welpott on photographs of women. The project culminated with an exhibition at George Eastman House in 1973 and a book, *Women and Other Visions*, published in 1975. I became a founding member of the Visual Dialogue Foundation, a group of San Francisco Bay Area photographers who met and exhibited together regularly. The group stayed together for several years but eventually disbanded, as members became too geographically scattered. After working as a photographer for seven years, I began to have my work included in some important group shows. The Visual Dialogue Foundation exhibited at the Lytton Center for Visual Arts in Oakland, California. The San Francisco Museum of Modern Art chose five photographers from this exhibition – Michael Bishop, Clyde Dilley, Leland Rice, John Spence Weir, and myself – for a show at the Museum. I moved to San Anselmo, California, a rustic little town in Marin County, north of San Francisco. I exhibited at the Witkin Gallery in New York City, again with some of the members of the Visual Dialogue Foundation: Leland Rice, John Spence Weir, and Jack Welpott.

1973-1974
My work was published in some major publications – first in *Photography Year 1973* (Time/Life) and *The Woman's Eye* by Anne Tucker (Alfred A. Knopf). These publications helped call attention to women in the medium. I participated with Lee Friedlander, Jerry Uelsmann and Jack Welpott, under the directorship of Lucien Clergue, in the first International Workshop in Photography, held in Arles, France. We were all awarded the Medal of Arles from the city. It was my first award of any kind and I remember the event with great fondness. In 1974 I was awarded the Dorothea Lange Award from the Oakland Museum for "outstanding contributions to photography by a woman."

1975-1977
The book *Women and Other Visions* was published in 1975. By now I was thought of as a photographer of women, even though I had temporarily stopped photographing women and begun working on other themes. I did a series

of room interiors and still lifes, and then moved on to do portraits and nudes of men. The series of photographs of men continued on through 1978. I was teaching various classes at the San Francisco Art Institute, and also traveling to do workshops and lectures.

1978-1980
I spent most of 1978 working on my book *Imogen Cunningham: A Portrait* (NYGS). Imogen had died in 1976 at the age of ninety-three. I interviewed and photographed various people who had known Imogen – her immediate family, other artists, historians, critics, and a wide range of friends. The book contained a portfolio of sixty of Imogen's images. It was a labor of love. Towards the end of the year I received news that I had been awarded a Guggenheim Fellowship. I completed my work on the book and in the summer of 1979 went to Egypt and Israel on my Guggenheim. I went again the following year to take more pictures, and spent time in both Egypt and Morocco. In between trips to Egypt, I traveled in the West and Southwest photographing. I began work on an extensive series of self-portraits. In August of 1980 I moved to Santa Fe, New Mexico.

1981-1982
I lived in Santa Fe and continued to work on my self-portraits and autobiographical work. It was a strange and isolating time for me, but also very productive. In the fall of 1982 I returned to California.

1983-1986
Once back in San Anselmo, I continued working on my autobiographical pieces. I incorporated writing into some of them, and made groupings of photographs. In 1984 I showed much of this work at the Grapestake Gallery in San Francisco. I was approached by Georgianna Lagoria from the De Saisset Museum, University of Santa Clara, to prepare a twenty-year retrospective of my work. The subsequent exhibition and book became a collaborative project between the De Saisset Museum and the University of Arizona. The book *Judy Dater: Twenty Years* included an essay by James Enyeart. The exhibition traveled to various places in the United States and to Barcelona. I began work on a book with writer Carolyn Coman. The book *Body & Soul* tells the stories of ten diverse and fascinating American women through photographs and interviews.

1987-1990
In January of 1987, I moved to New York City. The move brought on many changes, and I adjusted. I continued to live in New York, working on *Body & Soul*, teaching at the International Center of Photography, and began to do my large composite narrative pieces. *Body & Soul* was published by Hill & Co. In 1988, and I received my second National Endowment for the Arts Grant. I traveled back and forth between New York and California regularly. I loved the energy and cultural life of New York. I loved the beauty and comfort of California. I was invited to Japan by Toppan Printing Co., Ltd. to participate in a celebration of the 150th anniversary of photography with 11 other photographers from around the world. Towards the end of 1990, Sumner Stone, a type designer, visited me in New York. We had a date. We had a good conversation. I had a prophetic dream the next night.

1991-1994
I began to write my memoirs. I started to combine my words and my photographs with the aid of the computer. I moved back to California and Sumner and I were married. In 1992 I returned to Japan for the publication of the Japanese version of *Cycles,* and an accompanying exhibition in Tokyo. The exhibition will travel through 1996. I continue to photograph and work on the computer.

Bibliography

Selected One-Person Exhibitions

1995   *Cycles,* Honolulu Academy of Arts, Honolulu, Hawaii

1994   *Cycles,* International Center of Photography, New York, NY

1993   *Photographs and Installations* 1988-1992, Smith Anderson Gallery, Palo Alto, CA

1992   *Cycles.* Matsuya Department Store, Ginza, Tokyo, Japan

1991   *Judy Dater Photography.* Stockton State College Art Gallery, Pomona, NJ

1990   Options Gallery, Odessa College, Odessa, TX

1989   *Judy Dater, New Works.* Blatant Image/Silver Eye, Pittsburgh, PA
        Judy Dater, Recent Photographs. Santa Monica College, Santa Monica, CA

1988   *The Spirit of Woman, Judy Dater Photographs.* Albin O. Kuhn Library and Gallery, University of Maryland, Baltimore County, MD
        Recent and Rarely Seen Photographs, Judy Dater. Images Gallery, Cincinnati, OH

1986   *Judy Dater.* Webster University, St. Louis, MO
        Judy Dater: Twenty Years. DeSaisset Museum, University of Santa Clara, CA (Traveled)

1985   Northern Arizona University Art Gallery, Flagstaff, AZ

1984   Grapestake Gallery, San Francisco, CA
        Kathleen Ewing Gallery, Washington, DC
        Portraits of Disabled Artists. San Francisco, CA
        Museum of Modern Art, San Francisco, CA
        Yuen Lui Gallery, Seattle, WA

1983   North Carolina State University, Raleigh, NC
        Idaho State, Pocatello, ID
        Victor Hasselblad Aktiebolag Gallery, Goteborg, Sweden
        University of Oregon, University Art Museum, Eugene, OR
        The Photographic Center, Dallas, TX
        Lone Star Photographic Workshop, Austin, TX

1982   Lightworks/Film in the Cities, St. Paul, MN
        Kathleen Ewing Gallery, Washington, DC
        Baker Gallery, Kansas City, MO
        Burton Gallery, Toronto, Canada
        Yuen Lui Gallery, Seattle, WA
        Spectrum Gallery, Fresno, CA
        Catskill Center for Photography, Woodstock, NY

1981   Atlanta Gallery, Atlanta, GA
        Camera Obscura Gallery, Denver, CO
        Orange Coast College, Costa Mesa, CA
        University of North Dakota Art Gallery, Grand Forks, ND

1980   Jeb Gallery, Providence, RI
        Photography Southwest Gallery, Scottsdale, AZ

1979   G. Ray Hawkins Gallery, Los Angeles, CA
        Yuen Lui Gallery, Seattle, WA
        Kimball Art Center, Park City, UT
        Contemporary Art Center, New Orleans, LA

1978   Witkin Gallery, New York, NY

1977   Grapestake Gallery, San Francisco, CA
        Susan Spiritus Gallery, Newport Beach, CA

1976   Evergreen State College, Olympia, WA

1975   Spectrum Gallery, Tucson, AZ
        Silver Image Gallery, Seattle, WA

1974   Oakland Museum, Oakland, CA

1973   University of Colorado, Boulder, CO
        Center for Photographic Studies, Louisville, KY

1972   University of Maryland, Baltimore, MD
        Witkin Gallery, New York, NY

1965   Aardvark Gallery, San Francisco, CA

Selected Two-Person Exhibitions

With Imogen Cunningham:

1986   Gallery of Contemporary Art, University of Colorado, Colorado Springs, CO

With Gail Skoff:

1982   *Girls of the Golden West.* Santa Fe Center for Photography, Santa Fe, NM

With Jack Welpott:

1976   Galerie Fiolet, Amsterdam, The Netherlands
        University of Tokyo Gallery, Tokyo, Japan
        Musée Réattu, Arles, France
        Enjay Gallery, Boston, MA

1975   Shadai Gallery, Tokyo, Japan
        Washington Gallery of Photography, Washington, DC

1974   Witkin Gallery, New York, NY

1973   George Eastman House, Rochester, NY
        Focus Gallery, San Francisco, CA
        Image Works Gallery, Cambridge, MA
        Ohio Silver Gallery, Los Angeles, CA

Selected Group Exhibitions

1993   *In Progress,* San Francisco Art Institute,
        San Francisco, CA
1992   *The Reflective Eye,* Palm Springs Desert Museum,
        Palm Springs, CA
1991   *Identity Crisis: Portraits in the Eighties.*
        Center for Creative Photography,
        University of Arizona, Tucson, AZ*
        Women Viewing Women. Rockford College Art
        Gallery, Clark Arts Center, Rockford, IL
        To Collect the Art of Women. The Jane Reese
        Williams Photography Collection,
        Museum of Fine Arts, Museum of New Mexico,
        Santa Fe, NM (Traveled)*
        *Exploring the Unknown Self: Self-Portraits of
        Contemporary Women.* Tokyo Metropolitan
        Museum of Photography, Tokyo, Japan**
1990   *Photographs Updated: Similar Images/Dissimilar
        Motives.* Sonoma State University Art
        Gallery, Sonoma, CA*
        The Odalisque.
        Jayne Baum Gallery, New York, NY
1989   *Decade by Decade, Twentieth-Century American
        Photography.* From the Collection of the
        Center for Creative Photography,
        Phoenix Art Museum, Phoenix, AZ**
        Capturing an Image. Collecting 150 Years of
        Photography, Museum of Fine Arts, Fogg Art
        Museum, Harvard University, Boston, MA
        *Suburban Home Life: Tracking the American
        Dream.* Whitney Museum of American Art,
        New York, NY*
        *Popular and Preferred Imagery in American
        Photography.* Boca Raton Museum of Art,
        Boca Raton, FL**
        Self and Shadow. Burden Gallery, New York, NY*
        Picturing California.
        Oakland Museum, Oakland, CA**
        Light Years.
        University of Maryland, Baltimore, MD
        Coming of Age: Twenty-one Years of Collecting.
        Madison Art Center, Madison, WI
        Witness. Fuller Gross Gallery, San Francisco, CA
1988   *Portraits.* Purdue University, West Lafayette, IN*
        *Reflections: Woman's Self-Image in Contemporary
        Photography.* Miami University,
        Oxford, OH (Traveled)*
        Behold the Man: The Male Nude in Photography.
        Stills Gallery, Edinburgh, Scotland (Traveled)*
        Bay Area Masters Series.
        Triton Museum of Art, Santa Clara, CA*

*First Person Singular: Self-Portrait Photography
1840-1987.* High Museum, Atlanta, GA*
The M. Anwar Kamal Collection.
Cummer Gallery of Art, Jacksonville, FL*
1987   *Terra Cognita.* San Jose Institute
        of Contemporary Art, San Jose, CA*
        Contemporary American Figurative Photography.
        Center of the Arts, Miami, FL
        In a New Light.
        Catskill Center of Photography, Woodstock, NY*
        Earth Vision/Human Scale.
        The Woman's Building Gallery, Los Angeles, CA
        Reclaiming Paradise.
        Tweed Museum of Art, Duluth, MN (Traveled)*
1986   *Staging the Self: Self-Portrait Photography 1840s-
        1980s.* National Portrait Gallery,
        London, England (Traveled)
        Life Stories. MCAD Gallery, Los Angeles, CA
        With the Land. Sonoma State University Art
        Gallery, Sonoma, CA
        Commitment to Vision. University of Oregon
        Art Gallery, Eugene, OR (Traveled)*
        First Group Exhibition.
        Min Gallery, Tokyo, Japan*
1985   *Self as Subject.*
        Honolulu Academy of Arts, Honolulu, HI
        *This is Not about the Artist's Ego: Some Political
        Photographs of the 1980s.*
        Artemisia Gallery, Chicago, IL
        A Women's Show.
        Photographer's Gallery, Palo Alto, CA
1984   *Photography in California 1945-1980.*
        San Francisco Museum of Modern Art,
        San Francisco, CA (Traveled)**
        The Nude in Photography.
        Stadtmuseum, Munich, Germany*
        Faces Photographed. From the Permanent
        Collection, San Francisco Museum of
        Modern Art, San Francisco, CA*
        The Art of California.
        Selections from the Steinman Collection,
        Oakland Museum, Oakland, CA
        La Photographie Créative. Les Collections de
        Photographies Contemporaines de la
        Bibliothèque Nationale, Paris, France**
        101 Photographs. Selections from the Steinman
        Collection, Santa Barbara Museum of Art,
        Santa Barbara, CA
        The Naked Nude.
        San Francisco Art Institute, San Francisco, CA
        15th Anniversary. Witkin Gallery, New York, NY
        Attitudes and Expressions. Classic and

Contemporary Portrait Photography, Mills
House, Visual Arts Complex, Garden Grove, CA*

1983   *Subjective Vision.* The Lucinda W. Bunnen
Collection of Photographs,
High Museum of Art, Atlanta, GA*
The Arranged Image.
Boise Gallery of Art, Boise, ID*
Printed by Women.
Port of History Museum, Philadelphia, PA*
Discovering Photography.
Brockton Art Museum, Brockton, MA
Recent American Landscapes.
Baker Gallery, Kansas City, MO

1982   Heydt/Bair Gallery, Santa Fe, NM
American Photography Today.
University of Colorado, Denver, CO**
California Photography. Rhode Island
School of Design, Providence, RI*
Influences.
Second Street Gallery, Charlottesville, VA

1981   *A Sentimental Celebration.*
Focus Gallery, San Francisco, CA
Photo Facts and Opinions. Addison Gallery of
American Art, Andover, MA**
Portrait Styles: Judy Dater and Her Predecessors.
Catskill Center for Photography,
Woodstock, NY

1979   *Photography Als Kunst 1949-1979.*
Tiroler-Landesmuseum, Austria (Traveled)**
Attitudes: Photography in the Seventies. Santa
Barbara Museum of Art, Santa Barbara, CA*

1978   *Forty American Photographers.*
Crocker Art Museum, Sacramento, CA*
The Graham Nash Collection. DeSaisset Museum,
University of Santa Clara, Santa Clara, CA*
Mirrors and Windows. The Museum of Modern
Art, New York, NY (Traveled)**
Tusen Och en Bild.
Moderna Museet, Stockholm, Sweden*

1977   *Great West: Real/Ideal.* University of Colorado,
Boulder, CO (Traveled)**

1976   *Contemporary Trends.*
Columbia College, Chicago, IL (Traveled)*
U.C.L.A. Collection of Contemporary American
Photographs, Fredrick S. Wight Art Gallery,
University of California, Los Angeles, CA

1975   *Women of Photography: An Historical Survey.*
The San Francisco Museum of Modern Art,
San Francisco, CA (Traveled)**

1974   *Photography in America.* Whitney Museum
of American Art, New York, NY**
Private Realities: Recent American Photography.

Boston Museum of Fine Arts, Boston, MA**
New Images in Photography: Object and Illusion.
Lowe Art Museum, University of Miami, FL*

1973   *Sixties Continuum.* International Museum
of Photography, Rochester, NY**

1972   *Photographic Portraits.*
Moore College of Art, Philadelphia, PA
Photographs of Women.
Museum of Modern Art, New York, NY

1971   Visual Dialogue Foundation,
Friends of Photography, Carmel, CA

1970   *California Photographers 1970.*
Pasadena Art Museum, Pasadena, CA*
Being Without Clothes. Massachusetts Institute
of Technology, Cambridge, MA**

1969   *Vision and Expression.* International Museum
of Photography, Rochester, NY**
Visual Dialogue Foundation, Center of the
Visual Arts, Lytton Center, Oakland, CA

1968   *Light 7.* Hayden Gallery, Massachusetts
Institute of Technology, Cambridge, MA

1967   *Photography U.S.A.*
De Cordova Museum, Lincoln, MA

*Accompanying Catalogue   **Accompanying Book

Selected Permanent Collections

Addison Gallery of American Art,
Phillips Academy, Andover, MA
Albin O. Kuhn Library and Gallery,
University of Maryland, Baltimore, MD
Bayly Art Museum, University of Virginia
Bibliothèque Nationale, Paris, France
Boston Museum of Fine Arts, Boston, MA
Brookdale Community College, Lincroft, NJ
Center for Creative Photography, Tucson, AZ
Claremont Colleges Gallery,
Scripps College, Claremont, CA
Cleveland Museum of Art, Cleveland, OH
Detroit Institute of Arts, Detroit, MI
Federal Reserve Bank of San Francisco, San Francisco, CA
Fogg Art Museum, Harvard University,
Cambridge, MA
Hackley Art Museum, Muskegon, MI
Indiana University, Kinsey Institute for Sex Research,
Bloomington, IN
International Center for Photography, New York, NY
International Museum for Photography, Rochester, NY
Israel Museum, Jerusalem, Israel
Kalamazoo Institute of the Arts, Kalamazoo, MI

Library of Congress, Washington, DC
Reva and David Logan Foundation, Chicago, IL
Metropolitan Museum of Art, New York, NY
Milwaukee Art Center, Milwaukee, WI
Moderna Museet, Stockholm, Sweden
Museum of Fine Arts, Santa Fe, NM
Museum of Modern Art, New York, NY
Museum of Modern Art, San Francisco, CA
National Gallery of Canada, Ottawa, Canada
Newport Harbor Art Museum, Newport, CA
Oakland Museum, Oakland, CA
Phoenix College, Phoenix, AZ
Princeton University Art Museum, Princeton, NJ
Santa Barbara Museum of Art, Santa Barbara, CA
Seattle Art Museum, Seattle, WA
Norton Simon Museum of Art, Pasadena, CA
Smith College Museum of Art, Northhampton, MA
Toledo Museum of Art, Toledo, OH
Toppan Collection, Tokyo Metropolitan Museum of
Photography, Tokyo, Japan
University of California, Los Angeles, CA
University of Kansas, Lawrence, KS
University of Kentucky, Louisville, KY
University of Maryland, Baltimore, MD
University of Michigan, Ann Arbor, MI
University of New Mexico, Albuquerque, NM
University of Oklahoma, Norman, OK
Visual Studies Workshop, Rochester, NY
Virginia Museum of Fine Arts, Richmond, VA
Washington State University, Pullman, WA
Wellesley College Arts Center, Wellesley, MA
Yale University Art Gallery, New Haven, CT

Major Publications, Books

1994   *Cycles: Judy Dater.*
        Introduction by Sheryl Conkelton
        Foreword by Clarissa Pinkola Estés, Ph.D.
        Curatorial Assistance, Inc., Pasadena, CA
1992   *Cycles: Judy Dater.*
        Interview by Donna Stein. Essay by Michiko
        Kasahara. Kodansha, Tokyo, Japan
1988   *Body & Soul: Ten American Women.* Judy Dater
        & Carolyn Coman. Hill & Co., Boston, MA
1986   *Judy Dater: Twenty Years.* Essay by James Enyeart.
        University of Arizona Press
1979   *Imogen Cunningham: A Portrait.* Judy Dater.
        New York Graphic Society, Boston, MA
1975   *Women and Other Visions, Photographs by Judy
        Dater and Jack Welpott.* Introduction by
        Henry Holmes Smith. Morgan & Morgan

Selected Publications, Books

1990   *Fully Exposed: The Male Nude in Photography.*
        Emmanuel Cooper. Unwin Hyman Limited
        La Photographie à la Croisée, Iles Chemins.
        Pierre Borhan. La Manufacture
        Yellow Silk. Edited by Lily Pond & Richard Russo.
        Harmony Books
1989   *54 Master Photographers of 1960-1979.*
        Toppan Collection, Toppan Printing Co., Ltd.,
        Tokyo, Japan
        *Portrait and the Camera: A Celebration of 150 Years
        of Photography.* Robert Lassam Studio Editions,
        London, England
1988   *Master Photographs* from *'Photography in the Fine
        Arts' Exhibitions 1959-1967.* The International
        Center for Photography, New York, NY
1987   *The Naked and the Nude.* Jorge Lewinski.
        Weidenfeld and Nicolson, London, England
        Frauenbilder. Petra Olschewski. Edition
        Stemmle, Germany-Switzerland
        Das Verborgene Bild. Peter Weiermair.
        Ariadne, Germany
        Light Years 1967-1987. Untitled #43.
        The Friends of Photography, San Francisco, CA
1986   *50 Years of Modern Color Photography 1936-1986.*
        Photokina, Germany
        San Francisco Observed. Ruth Silverman.
        Chronicle Books, San Francisco, CA
        Contemporary American Photography.
        Part 1. Min Gallery, Tokyo, Japan
1985   *Masterpieces of Photography from the George
        Eastman House Collections.* Robert Sobieszek.
        Abbeville Press, New York, NY
        Das Aktfoto. Michael Kohler & Gisela Barch.
        Munchner Stadtmuseum
        Living with Art.
        McCarter/Gilbert. Alfred A. Knopf
        Photographers Encyclopedia International.
        Editions Camera Obscura,
        Hermance, Switzerland
1984   *A World History of Photography.* Naomi
        Rosenblum. Abbeville Press. New York, NY
        The Gallery of World Photography.
        Contemporary Trends, DNP (America) Inc.
        Photograph., 3rd Edition.
        Upton & Upton. Little Brown & Co.
        The Art of Photography: Image & Illusion.
        Gene Markowski. University of Virginia,
        Prentice-Hall Inc., Englewood Cliffs, NJ
        American Photography: A Critical History.
        Jonathan Green. Harry N. Abrams,

New York, NY
Der Erotische Augenblick. Freyermuth/Fabian.
Stern Bibliothek der Fotografie,
Hamburg, Germany
Friends and Strange Dreams: Photographs by Wah Lui. Introduction by Judy Dater.
Distant Thunder Press, Seattle, WA

1982 *Contemporary Photographers*. St. Martins Press
1980 *Contact Theory*. Lustrum Press, New York, NY
1979 *The Photograph Collector's Guide.*
Lee D. Witkin and Barbara London,
New York Graphic Society, Boston, MA
A Ten Year Salute. Lee D. Witkin. Addison House
Light Readings. A.D. Coleman. Oxford Press
1978 *Darkroom II*. Jane Kelly.
Lustrum Press, New York, NY
1977 *Faces: A Narrative History of the Portrait in Photography*. Ben Maddow. New York Graphic
Society, A Chanticleer Press Edition, Boston, MA
1973 *The Woman's Eye*. Anne Tucker.
Knopf, New York, NY
Photography Year 1973. Time/Life Books

Selected Publications, Magazines and Journals

1993 *ZYZZYVA*, Vol. IX, #3 Fall 1993
1992 *Aperture, 40th Anniversary,* #129, Fall 1992
1992 *ZYZZYVA*, Vol. VIII, #3 Fall 1992
1992 *F2 Women in Photography*, Winter 1992
1991 *The Archive: 29*, Center for Creative Photography
1989 *Darkroom Photography*, 2:10, October 1989
Photo Paper, a Publication of Blatant
Image/Silver Eye, Spring 1989
Elle, 6:9, May 1989
1986 *American Photographer*, 17:6, December 1986
1985 *Woman's Art Journal*, 6:2, Fall 85/Winter 86
ZYZZYVA, 1:1, Spring 1985
ZYZZYVA, 1:2, Summer 1985
Cliches, 20:19, September 1985
1984 *Aperture: Minor White - A Living Remembrance*,
#95, Summer 1984
Artweek, Mar. 31, 1984
Foto, 1984, #9
1983 *Polaroid Close-Up*, 14:1, April 1983
Darkroom Photography, 5:7, November 1983
Aktuell Fotografi, December 1983
Popular Photography, 90:2, February 1983
1981 *Photographer's Forum*, 3:4, September 1981
The Archive, #14, December 1981
Modern Photography, 45:4, May 1981
1980 *Art New England*, 1:7, June 1980

1979 *Picture Magazine*, #11, April 1979
Artforum, 17:5, January 1979
Village Voice, 24:5, June 29, 1979
G. Ray Hawkins Gallery Photo Bulletin, 2:8,
December 1979
1978 *Ms. Magazine*, 6:12, June 1978
Artweek, 9:39, November 18, 1978
1976 *Artforum*, September 1976
Art in America, 64:1, January/February, 1976
Esquire, 85:2, February, February 1976
1975 *Zoom Magazine*, #29, 1975
Camera Magazine, October 1975
Artweek, October 11, 1975
1974 *The New York Times*, April 14, 1974, sect. 2, p.30
Untitled Quarterly, 7/8, 1974,
Friends of Photography, San Francisco, CA
1973 *Place Magazine*, 3:1, June 1973
Image, 16:1, March 1973, George Eastman House
1972 *The New York Times*, June 4, 1972, sect. 2, p:16
1970 *Album Magazine*, October 1970
Camera, 49:4, April 1970
San Francisco Camera, 1969-70
Aperture, 1968-1970

Grants and Awards
1988 National Endowment for the Arts,
Individual Artist Grant
1987 Marin Arts Council Individual Artist Grant
1978 Guggenheim Fellowship
1976 National Endowment for the Arts,
Individual Artist Grant
1974 Dorothea Lange Award, Oakland Museum

Films
1981 *The Woman Behind the Image: Photographer Judy Dater*. John Stewart Productions,
16 mm, 27 minutes, color/sound

Live Performance
1983 *En Abyme* with Sam Samore at La Mamelle,
San Francisco, CA

Limited Edition Portfolios
1981 *The Image Continuum*. Journal Five, Eugene, OR
Men/Women. Collected Visions,
San Francisco, CA Ed. 60
1973 *Ten Photographs*. Witkin/Berley,
New York, NY Ed. 25
1970 Founders Portfolio. Visual Dialogue
Foundation, San Francisco, CA

Chronological List of Photographs

101. Lovers #1, 1964. Silver print,
9⅛ x 7⅛ (23.1 x 18 cm)

102. Lovers #2, 1964. Silver print,
9⅛ x 7⅛ (23.1 x 18 cm)

26. Untitled (Alabaster statue), 1964.
Silver print, 13⅛ x 10⁹⁄₁₆ (33 x 26.8 cm)

2. Self-portrait, 1965. Silver print,
13⅜ x 10⅜ (34 x 26.3 cm)

103. Embrace, 1965. Silver print,
9⅜ x 7½ (23.8 x 19 cm)

31. Dead deer in pond, 1966. Silver print,
7⁷⁄₁₆ x 9⁵⁄₁₆ (18.9 x 23.6 cm)

98. Priest, Tomales, California, 1966. Silver print,
9½ x 7½ (24.1 x 19 cm)

104. Legion of Honor, 1966. Silver print,
7⅜ x 9⁵⁄₁₆ (18.7 x 23.6 cm)

105. At Napoleon's tomb, Paris, 1967. Silver print,
6¹⁵⁄₁₆ x 4⅝ (17.6 x 11.7 cm)

99. The voyeur, 1968. Silver print,
7⁷⁄₁₆ x 9⁵⁄₁₆ (18.9 x 23.6 cm)

58. Pregnant dream, 1968-69.
Hand-painted silver print, 6⅜ x 5⅛ (16.1 x 13 cm)

106. Aspen, 1969. Silver print,
7⅝ x 7⁹⁄₁₆ (19.4 x 19.2 cm)

107. Joyce Goldstein, 1969. Silver print,
18½ x 14½ (47 x 36.8 cm)

20. Twinka Thiebaud, actress, model, 1970.
Silver print, 18½ x 14½ (47 x 36.8 cm)

108. Maria Moreno, 1971. Silver print,
8⁷⁄₁₆ x 7¾ (21.4 x 19.7 cm)

109. Gael and Rachel, 1971. Silver print,
13⁷⁄₁₆ x 10⅜ (34.1 x 26.3 cm)

110. Maria and Legend, 1971. Silver print,
9⁵⁄₁₆ x 7⁵⁄₁₆ (23.6 x 18.6 cm)

25. Libby, 1971. Silver print,
13¼ x 10½ (33.6 x 26.7 cm)

113. Woman in white, Bloomington, Indiana, 1971.
Silver print, 7⁷⁄₁₆ x 7⁹⁄₁₆ (18.9 x 19.2 cm)

39. Prayer, 1971. Silver print,
7⁷⁄₁₆ x 9⁷⁄₁₆ (24 x 18.9 cm)

111. Afternoon in Danville, 1971. Silver print,
9⁵⁄₁₆ x 7⁷⁄₁₆ (23.6 x 18.9 cm)

112. Danville bedroom, 1971. Silver print,
9⁵⁄₁₆ x 7⁷⁄₁₆ (23.6 x 18.9 cm)

24. Aarmour Starr, 1972. Silver print,
13⁷⁄₁₆ x 10⅜ (34.1 x 26.3 cm)

114. Gwen, 1972.

Silver print, 9¼ x 7¼ (23.5 x 18.4 cm)

36. Gwen (torso), 1972. Silver print,
13½ x 10⅜ (34.3 x 26.3 cm)

115. Kathleen Kelly, 1972. Silver print,
18½ x 14½ (47 x 36.8 cm)

42. Maureen with fan, 1972. Silver print,
9½ x 7½ (24 x 19 cm)

92. Lucia, 1972. Silver print,
9½ x 7½ (24 x 19 cm)

117. Cheri, 1972. Silver print,
10½ x 13½ (26.7 x 34.3 cm)

116. Valerie, 1972. Silver print,
9⁵⁄₁₆ x 7⁷⁄₁₆ (23.6 x 18.9 cm)

22. Marianne with mask, 1972. Silver print,
9⁵⁄₁₆ x 7⁷⁄₁₆ (23.6 x 18.9 cm)

118. Maureen in mirror, 1972. Silver print,
10 x 12½ (25.4 x 31.7 cm)

27. Kathleen and China, 1972. Silver print,
9½ x 7 (24.1 x 17.8 cm)

121. Daydreams, 1973. Silver print,
10⅜ x 13⅜ (26.3 x 34 cm)

16. Self-portrait, Arles, France, 1973.
Silver print, 17¾ x 14⅛ (45.1 x 35.9 cm)

124. Bedroom, Arles, France, 1973.
Silver print, 13½ x 10½ (34.3 x 26.7 cm)

123. Wally and Nadine, 1973. Silver print,
7½ x 9⅜ (19 x 23.8 cm)

40. Jack with monkey, 1973. Silver print,
9⁵⁄₁₆ x 7⁷⁄₁₆ (23.6 x 18.9 cm)

119. Fantasy in black and white, 1973. Silver print,
6½ x 5⁵⁄₁₆ (16.5 x 13.5 cm)

122. Laura Mae, 1973. Silver print,
18½ x 14½ (47 x 36.8 cm)

120. Imogen in the mirror, 1973. Silver print,
5⁵⁄₁₆ x 6¾ (13 x 17.1 cm)

126. Maria Theresa, 1974. Silver print,
13⅜ x 10⅜ (34 x 26.3 cm)

125. Kelly and Sybil, 1974. Silver print,
9³⁄₁₆ x 7¹⁵⁄₁₆ (23.3 x 20.1 cm)

100. Imogen and Twinka at Yosemite, 1974.
Silver print, 13½ x 10½ (34.3 x 26.7 cm)

32. Summer bath, 1975. Silver print,
10½ x 13½ (26.7 x 34.3 cm)

127. Sandy, 1975. Silver print,
13½ x 10½ (34.3 x 26.7 cm)

21. Nehemiah, 1975. Silver print,
18 x 23 (45.7 x 58.4 cm)

91. Minor White, 1975. Silver print,
13½ x 10½ (34.3 x 26.7 cm)

94. Linda's Dream, 1975. Silver print,
13⅜ x 10⅜ (34 x 26.3 cm)

95. Double heart tree, 1975. Silver print,
10⁵⁄₁₆ x 13⁵⁄₁₆ (26.2 x 33.8 cm)

93. Linda and blackbird, 1975. Silver print,
9⁵⁄₁₆ x 7⁷⁄₁₆ (23.6 x 18.9 cm)

97. John Gutmann, 1975. Silver print,
6¹¹⁄₁₆ x 5⁵⁄₁₆ (17 x 13.5 cm)

38. Chris, 1975. Silver print,
9½ x 7⁹⁄₁₆ (24.1 x 19.2 cm)

128. Repose of the deposed, 1975.
Silver print, 9⅜ x 7⅜ (23.8 x 18.7 cm)

89. Postmen, Arles, 1976. Silver print,
13½ x 10½ (34.3 x 26.7 cm)

129. Stairs, Mexico, 1976. Silver print,
9⅜ x 7⁷⁄₁₆ (23.8 x 18.9 cm)

87. Man with bull dogs, New York, 1976.
Silver print, 13½ x 10½ (34.3 x 26.7 cm)

131, 132, 133, 134, 135, 136, 137.
Arles Suite, 1976-78.
Seven silver prints, 6¼ x 9⅛ each
(23.2 x 15.9 cm)

90. Peter Bunnell, 1977. Silver print,
18½ x 14½ (47 x 36.8 cm)

130. Bedroom window with fan, 1977.
Silver print, 9⅜ x 7½ (23.8 x 19 cm)

37. Walter Chappell, 1977. Silver print,
17¾ x 14⅛ (45.1 x 35.9 cm)

88. Solo, Hawaii, 1978. Silver print,
9⁵⁄₁₆ x 7⁷⁄₁₆ (23.6 x 18.9 cm)

41. Edmund Teske, 1978. Silver print,
7⅜ x 9⁷⁄₁₆ (18.7 x 24 cm)

140. Bernie, 1978. Silver print,
13½ x 10½ (34.3 x 26.7 cm)

139. Hide, 1978. Silver print,
13½ x 10½ (34.3 x 26.7 cm)

138. Patrick Nagatani, 1978. Silver print,
13½ x 10½ (34.3 x 26.7 cm)

81. Chris with tea cup, 1978. Type C print,
13½ x 10½ (34.3 x 26.7 cm)

80. Nude at Ship Rock, 1979. Type C print,
15½ x 19½ (39.3 x 49.5 cm)

78. Man with horse's skull, 1979.
Type C print, 19½ x 15½ (49.5 x 39.3 cm)

79. Man at pond, Tuscarora, Nevada, 1979.
Type C print, 15½ x 19½ (39.3 x 49.5 cm)

84. Ralph with radish, 1979. Type C print,
9½ x 7½ (24 x 19 cm)

7. Self-portrait with mist, 1980.
Silver print, 23¼ x 18 (59 x 45.7 cm)

14. Self-portrait with sparkler, 1980.
Silver print, 19½ x 15½ (49.5 x 39.3 cm)

1. My hands, Death Valley, 1980. Silver print,
15½ x 19½ (39.3 x 49.5 cm)

96. Consuelo Cloos, 1980. Silver print,
13½ x 10½ (34.3 x 26.7 cm)

85. Kamal El Mallakh, 1980. Type C print,
13½ x 10½ (34.3 x 26.7 cm)

141. Salah Jahine, Cairo, 1980. Silver print,
18½ x 14½ (47 x 36.8 cm)

83. Bill Justima, 1980. Type C print,
13½ x 10½ (34.3 x 26.7 cm)

142. Man with bird, Pittsburgh, 1981.
Silver print, 13¼ x 10¼ (33.6 x 26.2 cm)

17. Self-portrait with mask, 1981.
Silver print, 15½ x 19½ (39.3 x 49.5 cm)

8. Self-portrait in grasslands, 1981.
Silver print, 15½ x 19½ (39.4 x 49.5 cm)

6. Self-portrait, Craters of the Moon, 1981.
Silver print, 15½ x 19½ (39.4 x 49.5 cm)

11. Self-portrait with stone, 1981. Silver print,
18 x 23¼ (45.7 x 59 cm)

9. Self-portrait, Badlands, 1981. Silver print,
15½ x 19½ (39.4 x 49.5 cm)

5. Self-portrait with parents, 1981. Silver print,
19½ x 15½ (49.5 x 39.4 cm)

15. Self-portrait with petroglyph, 1981.
Silver print, 19½ x 15½ (49.5 x 39.3 cm)

10. Self-portrait at Salt Flats, 1981.
Silver print, 15½ x 19½ (39.4 x 49.6 cm)

143. Gail with rain, 1982. Silver print,
7⁷⁄₁₆ x 9¼ (18.9 x 23.5 cm)

3. Self-portrait with rain, 1982. Silver print,
10⅞ x 9³⁄₁₆ (27.6 x 23.3 cm)

18. Self-portrait on deserted road, 1982.
Silver print, 15½ x 19½ (39.4 x 49.5 cm)

19. Cat woman, 1982. Silver print,
13½ x 10½ (34 .3 x 26.7 cm)

67. All American nude, 1982, Type C print,
19½ x 15½ (49.5 x 39.4 cm)

62. Spider woman, 1982. Type C print,
19½ x 15½ (49.5 x 39.4 cm)

61. Elephant woman steps out, 1982.
Type C print, 19½ x 15½ (49.5 x 39.4 cm)

64. Death by ironing, 1982. Type C print,
19½ x 15½ (49.5 x 39.4 cm)

68. Self-portrait with Bugs Bunny, 1982.
Type C print, 19½ x 15½ (49.5 x 39.4 cm)

57. Self-portrait with party dress, 1982.
Type C print, 19½ x 15½ (49.5 x 39.4 cm)

66. The magician, 1982. Type C print,
19½ x 15½ (49.5 x 39.4 cm)

63. Scream, 1982. Type C print,
19½ x 15½ (49.5 x 39.4 cm)

60. Queen of the night, 1982. Type C print,
19½ x 15½ (49.5 x 39.4 cm)

65. Eating, 1982. Type C print,
19½ x 15½ (49.5 x 39.4 cm)

77. Viewing Mt. Rushmore, 1982.
Type C print, 9½ x 7½ (24.1 x 19 cm)

71. Teenage Diary, 1982. Twelve Type C prints,
9½ x 7½ each (24.1 x 19 cm)

72. Teenage Diary (detail), 1982. Type C print,
9½ x 7½ (24.1 x 19 cm)

12. Self-portrait with white rock, 1983.
Silver print, 15½ x 19½ (39.4 x 49.5 cm)

13. Self-portrait holding up rock, 1983.
Silver print, 15½ x 19½ (39.4 x 49.5 cm)

82. Mark Johnstone, 1983. Type C print,
13½ x 10½ (34.3 x 26.7 cm)

59. Oracle, 1984. Three Type C prints,
37¾ x 23¾ each (95.9 x 60.3 cm)

73. Love Letters #3 1984. Four Type C prints,
10½ x 10½ each (26.7 x 26.7 cm)

74. Love Letters #3 (detail). Type C print,
10½ x 10½ (26.7 x 26.7 cm)

75. Love Letters #3 (detail). Type C print,
10½ x 10½ (26.7 x 26.7 cm)

144. Woman with bomb #4, 1984. Silver print,
10½ x 13½ (34.3 x 26.7 cm)

145. Woman with bomb #2, 1984. Silver print,
10½ x 13½ (34.3 x 26.7 cm)

69. Fourth of July, State #4, 1984. Photolithograph,
30 x 21⅞ (76.2 x 55.6 cm)

146. Waterfall, North Carolina. 1985. Silver print,
9⅛ x 13½ (23.2 x 34.3 cm)

23. Belle de Jour, 1986. Silver print,
13⅜ x 9¹¹⁄₁₆ (33.8 x 24.6 cm)

28. Maggie in church, 1986. Silver print,
13⅜ x 10⁷⁄₁₆ (33.9 x 26.5 cm)

86. Vicki Singer, 1986. Silver print,
13⁷⁄₁₆ x 10⁷⁄₁₆ (34.1 x 26.5 cm)

43. Memory #1, 1987. Six silver prints,
48 x 60 (152.4 x 121.9 cm)

44. Memory #2, 1988. Six silver prints,
48 x 60 (152.4 x 121.9 cm)

45. Memory #4, 1988. Six silver prints,
48 x 60 (152.4 x 121.9 cm)

147. He won't be "first adulterer" president #1, 1988.
Silver print, 19⅛ x 12¾ (48.6 x 32.4 cm)

148. He won't be "first adulterer" president #2, 1988.
Silver print, 19⅛ x 12¾ (48.6 x 32.4 cm)

35. Offering #1, 1988. Silver print,
23¼ x 18 (59 x 45.7 cm)

29. Stephania, 1988. Silver print,
18¼ x 14¼ (46.3 x 36.3 cm)

46. The city, 1989. Six silver prints,
72 x 80 (182.9 x 203.2 cm)

48. Playing with fire, 1989. Nine silver prints,
72 x 60 (182.9 x 152.4 cm)

49. End of innocence, 1989. Nine silver prints,
72 x 60 (182.9 x 152.4 cm)

47. The meaning of life, 1989. Two silver prints,
24 x 40 (61 x 101.6 cm)

50. Cycles, 1989. Nine color polaroid prints,
72 x 60 (182.9 x 152.4 cm)

51. Cycles (detail), 1989. Color polaroid print,
24 x 20 (61 x 50.8 cm)

52. Cycles (detail), 1989. Color polaroid print,
24 x 20 (61 x 50.8 cm)

53. Blue angel, 1990. Three color polaroid prints,
28½ x 66 (72.4 x 167.6 cm)

54. The pond, 1990. Three color polaroid prints,
72 x 20 (182.9 x 50.8 cm)

55. The pond (detail), 1990. Color polaroid print
24 x 20 (61 x 50.8 cm)

56. Child/Woman, 1991. Computer image,
9¼ x 7⅜ (23.5 x 18.7 cm)

76. I didn't want to but I did, 1991.
Computer image, 10 x 6¼ (25.4 x 15.9 cm)

70. New York window, 1991. Computer image,
10 x 8 (25.4 x 20.3 cm)

150. Honeymoon, 1991. Silver print,
9⁷⁄₁₆ x 6¼ (24 x 15.9 cm)

4. Self-portrait Patmos, 1991. Silver print,
9⁷⁄₁₆ x 6¼ (24 x 15.9 cm)

34. Double trouble, Paris, 1991. Silver print,
9⁷⁄₁₆ x 6¼ (24 x 15.9 cm)

33. Male nude in mirror with hat, 1991.
Silver print, 9⅜ x 6¼ (23.8 x 15.9 cm)

149. In the brambles, Japan, 1991. Silver print,
6¼ x 9⁷⁄₁₆ (15.9 x 24 cm)

30. Japanese bath, 1991. Silver print,
9⁷⁄₁₆ x 6¼ (24 x 15.9 cm)